Get Out,
Explore, and
Have Fun!

June, 2010
Have Fun!

Falmouth, MA

of related interest

The Complete Guide to Asperger's Syndrome
Tony Attwood
ISBN 978 1 84310 495 7 (hardback)
ISBN 978 1 84310 669 2 (paperback)

Freaks, Geeks and Asperger Syndrome
A User Guide to Adolescence
Luke Jackson
Foreword by Tony Attwood
ISBN 978 1 84310 098 0

Kids in the Syndrome Mix of ADHD, LD, Asperger's, Tourette's, Bipolar, and More!
The One Stop Guide for Parents, Teachers, and Other Professionals
Martin L. Kutscher MD
With a contribution from Tony Attwood
With a contribution from Robert R Wolff MD
ISBN 978 1 84310 810 8 (hardback)
ISBN 978 1 84310 811 5 (paperback)

Hints and Tips for Helping Children with Autism Spectrum Disorders
Useful Strategies for Home, School, and the Community
Dion E. Betts and Nancy J. Patrick
ISBN 978 1 84310 896 2

Get Out, Explore, and Have Fun!

How Families of Children with Autism or Asperger Syndrome Can Get the Most out of Community Activities

Lisa Jo Rudy

Jessica Kingsley Publishers
London and Philadelphia

First published in 2010
by Jessica Kingsley Publishers
116 Pentonville Road
London N1 9JB, UK
and
400 Market Street, Suite 400
Philadelphia, PA 19106, USA

www.jkp.com

Library of Congress Cataloging in Publication Data
A CIP catalog record for this book is available from the Library of Congress

British Library Cataloguing in Publication Data
A CIP catalogue record for this book is available from the British Library

ISBN 978 1 84905 809 4

Printed and bound in the United States by
Thomson-Shore, Dexter, MI

For my son Tom, who has helped me
see how wide the world really is

Acknowledgments

Special thanks to the following families with children on the autism spectrum for sharing their stories and photos for this book:

David Greenberg, Marisol Villamil and their daughters Lena and Anna; Susan Senator, Ned Batchelder and their son Nathaniel; Stan and Judy Jaskiewicz and their son Peter; The Lai, Zlatin and Heiligman families and their sons Joshua Lai, Tyler Zlatin and David Heiligman; Jon Shestack, Portia Iversen and their son Dov; Nancy Wiseman and her daughter Sarah; John Elder Robison and his son Cubby (Jack); Sandy and Glenn Hartranft and their son "who teaches us everyday how to enjoy every moment"; Robin Cruz and her two sons; Julie Fuch and her son; Sean and Beth Homand and their son.

Special thanks to those individuals who took time out to tell me about their knowledge and experience. Your insights have helped to make this book a rich resource for getting out, exploring, and having fun!

Stephen Shore, Donna Williams, Cindy Schneider, Wendy Partridge, Jacquie Genovese, Anne Masters, Joe Harrington, Frank Ramirez, Bill Gaventa, and Kit Wilhite.

Contents

Preface

We're a family of four, including one child with an autism-spectrum diagnosis. We're not warriors, saviors, or miracle workers. We are, in fact, an average family. We do all the ordinary things that families do—trips to the beach and the zoo, sports and clubs for our kids, occasional adult-only evenings for us.

Like any parents, we're proud of our kids.

Of course, we're proud of our "neurotypical" daughter, who's a terrific soccer goalie, a budding entrepreneur, and a social butterfly.

We're also proud of our son Tom, diagnosed at age three with pervasive developmental disorder, not otherwise specified (PDD-NOS), officially part of the autism spectrum. We're not just proud of his ability to overcome autism's challenges: we're actually, honestly, proud of his achievements as a human being. We're proud when we see him fearlessly take the stage and perform on his clarinet. We're proud when he wins a bowling trophy. We're proud when he takes second prize for his artwork at the County Fair.

You might assume that Tom is so high functioning that his autism is not a serious issue. In fact, though, he has plenty of challenges. At age three, he was asked to leave two different preschools because of his language delays and unusual behaviors; at age eight, it became clear that he needed a specialized autism classroom; and at age ten, we decided to homeschool him. If you met Tom, it would take you only a minute or two to notice the differences in his speech patterns, social interactions, and movements that suggest "something is off." He has serious problems with social communication; so far, his best and only "true" friend is his younger sister.

How is it that our son has done so much, achieved so much, and made us so proud? We simply decided not to allow autism to get in the way of getting out, exploring, and having fun with our children. The results have been inspirational—not because our son is now a sports star or virtuoso but because he has discovered strengths, interests, and abilities that make his life (and ours) a whole lot of fun. We don't know, of course, whether Tom's present interests will take him toward a career, but like most fond parents, we dream.

How we rediscovered our (autistic) child

From the moment Tommy started showing signs of "differentness" (at almost three years old), we started to feel like outcasts in our own community.

First, his preschool, a homey little program at a church around the corner, told us he might do better in a different setting (another way of saying "please leave"). Then, a second preschool—one that claimed to address every child's unique needs—sent us packing. Their reason was that Tom had thrown a sweater at a teacher. The teacher had been a friend, and she was a member of our church. In one blow, we felt we'd lost both the school and the church. We tried to stick it out at church for a while, but the pitying smiles and the kind words of sympathy were the final straw.

As far as we were concerned, our son hadn't changed. He was still warm, funny, and smart. He was still talented, with great potential. He certainly didn't seem to us like "damaged goods."

Yes, our son had a diagnosis, and, yes, he needed various therapies. But as we sat outside (or inside) therapists' offices, listening to talk of ABA, RDI, AIT, GFCF, NVLD, OCD, and strategies for managing "stims" and "meltdowns," we found ourselves sinking deeper into a sense of disconnectedness. We knew why parents were so focused on therapy, but we just couldn't find it in ourselves to dedicate ourselves to a life of remediation.

Surely, we thought, we could live our lives—at least some of the time—outside the box of autism.

By good luck, as it turns out, we are museum professionals. My husband Peter and I met in a science museum, and we both worked (and work) for museums and science institutions. And so, without thinking much about it, we brought Tom along to see new exhibits we'd worked on, visit friends at the primate house at the zoo, and explore the aquarium when the giant shark tank was reinstalled.

At the museum, as we did everywhere, we did our best to keep Tom engaged and involved with his environment. From early on, we used a therapeutic approach called "floortime." The basic premise of floortime is that kids learn to interact through the process of "closing circles of communication." Simply put, through following the child's lead in play and exploration, you try to build up the number of meaningful back-and-forth interactions, with the goal of developing real communication and conversation.

It was easy to do floortime at the museum. There was so much to engage our eyes, ears, hands, bodies, and minds, so many different ways to communicate, and so many opportunities to play. In fact, we didn't think of it as therapy most of the time; to us, it was mostly just fun.

One day, we were at The Franklin Institute Science Museum in Philadelphia, our home away from home. A friend had created a new exhibit focused on supporting early-childhood development, so, of course, we were there on opening weekend. Tom, who had almost no real language skills outside of echolalia (repeating scripts learned from television and videos), was enchanted by the two-story ship, the lighthouse with the real light, and the walk-through cave.

I tried practicing floortime techniques with Tom in the gallery, but as it turned out, I didn't have to go it alone. Another little boy was playing with a two-sided magnetic maze that was designed to require two sets of hands. Tom sat down opposite the boy and started to play. He had never taken the initiative in this way, and we parents just stood back and watched. Together, wordlessly, the two boys worked their way through the maze—and then each went his own way. We smiled at the other boy's dad; he smiled back.

Things went equally well as we boarded the "boat," and Tom tried out various two-person, interactive exhibits. It took almost no encouraging at all to engage him in a perfectly ordinary manner with other (typically developing) kids. He used a forced-air device to send balls shooting through tubes, "sailed" a ship, and experimented with an interactive, bubble-making device. He didn't say much, but then again, he didn't have to. And other moms and dads seemed perfectly at ease with our son, who behaved—almost for the first time—just like any other five-year-old boy.

Our success at the museum was a great first step into the wide world. Soon, we were experimenting with all kinds of settings and situations. Some (classical concerts featuring musicians from the Philadelphia Orchestra) were a roaring success. Unlike other kids his age (then about eight), Tom loves classical music. Even as a little one, he could sit still and listen for a full hour. Other experiments (soccer, for example) were disastrous.

Tom is now 13. Over the years, we've found that a child with autism may have interests, abilities, and skills that are completely outside the cultural norm. What that means is that the typical activities of childhood—team sports and play dates—really can be tough. And that can be hard on a family. After all, most dads connect with their sons over sports. They build relationships with other dads through coaching teams or perhaps through leading a Scout pack (more on that later). Most moms connect with their children and one another through social activities like play dates, birthday parties, and carpooling. Most of those avenues are difficult to traverse with an autistic child.

But Tom's dad, Peter, is not particularly sports-oriented, so a terrific "guys' day out" for Tom and Peter became a family-oriented classical concert followed by lunch at the art museum and a trip through the galleries. Granted the experience was almost always the same (Tom had memorized the galleries and always took the same route). But how many dads can say their eight-year-old has an appreciation for Mozart *and* Picasso?

For me, the idea of kids and adults relating to one another "out of the box" has become an area of fascination. Over and over again, I watch as kids on the autism spectrum connect with the world, with typical individuals, and with one another in positive and unexpected ways. Sometimes, words are used. Sometimes they aren't. But the communication is real.

Unlike therapeutic settings in which artificial interactions are set up based on external goals, people in the real world interact over true mutual interests. Kids with autism, in the real world, can share their true interests with people who really, honestly care. Where there are real shared interests, there's real engagement, real interaction, and real learning. Where there's real learning and understanding, there's real respect. Where there's respect, there's the possibility of responsibility, leadership, and growth.

Whether your child with autism is verbal or nonverbal, whether he loves dinosaurs or baseball, there are other people out there with his passions. Not every setting is ideal for every child, and it takes work to find the right place, the right people, and the right situation. But when you encourage a child with autism to explore the world outside school and therapy, the results can be extraordinary.

Chapter 1

Getting Out, Exploring, and Having Fun: Why Does it Matter?

If you're the parent of a child or children with autism, you've probably read some dire "statistics" about the rate of divorce (rumored, but not proven, to be 85%). You may have heard that many families with kids on the autism spectrum spend up to $70,000 a year on therapies, thereby bankrupting themselves and depriving their other children. You almost certainly have heard about "warrior moms" (and dads) who spend most of their time confronting doctors, teachers, administrators, and therapists in support of therapies or programs they feel are best for their child. You've read or heard about controversies over vaccines, special diets, special education, autism treatments, and autism "wars."

In this book, you'll be reading about none of these issues.

That's because kids with autism—and their parents, brothers, sisters, and neighbors—are more than a collection of symptoms and challenges. They're people, with strengths and weaknesses, talents and abilities, humor and pathos. Like you, your child with autism needs to experience life. And like your child with autism, you, too, need an opportunity to stretch your wings.

This book is dedicated to the idea that getting out, exploring, and having fun with your child on the autism spectrum is important—to your child, to you, and to your family. In fact, getting out into the real world and participating in community activities may be even more important to your child's future (and yours) than trying yet another therapeutic avenue. After all, the whole point of all the therapies, treatments, and coaching is to provide your child with the tools to get out there and enjoy life. If he never actually leaves the house (except to go to school or visit the therapist, doctor, or social-skills group), he'll never have the chance to reap the fruit of those labors. What's more, your child will never have the chance to get to know his community; nor will your community have a chance to know—and love—your child.

Why "typicalness" lessons and school-based learning aren't enough

Many parents, teachers, and therapists think of community activities for autistic children as a nice extra. After autistic kids have learned to behave typically through therapy and gained the skills to learn and engage like typical students, they may earn the right to take part in music, art, nature, or community activities. Until and unless they behave like their typically developing peers, though, children with autism may even be denied the ordinary opportunities that other students routinely receive, like taking part in excursions to the zoo, the aquarium, the park, or the nature center.

Yet, for children with autism, the goal of "typicalness" may be permanently out of reach. Meanwhile, informal learning experiences may well turn out to be the key to self-discovery, communication, self-confidence, and even independence. That's because these nonschool settings have, for decades, embraced the idea that education takes many and varied forms. In fact, professional visitor-study organizations have reviewed, codified, and assessed the impact of hands-on, inquiry-based learning for children, teens, and families and found it to be extraordinarily valuable across the board.

In 1983, Dr. Howard Gardner's book *Frames of Mind: The Theory of Multiple Intelligence* presented to the wider world what many educators already knew: people learn differently. Gardner was among the first contemporary theorists to propose the idea that visual, kinesthetic, and aural experience can be as effective as traditional verbal and abstract instruction. The theory, stated simply, suggests that there are as many as nine different "intelligences," all of which provide avenues to learning. For autistic children, certain "intelligences," including visual, musical, natural, and numeric, tend to be most prevalent, while others (verbal and social) are least prevalent.

Gardner has gone on to do a wide range of research projects and to put many of his findings into practice. His idea of multiple intelligences has become a part of the pedagogical landscape, and in many schools, there really are opportunities for children to learn in many ways. Of course, Gardner's ideas are not absolutely unique: Montessori, Waldorf, and other educational visionaries have been using multisensory educational techniques for well over 100 years. Gardner was among the first, however, to bring this idea into the educational mainstream. His theories, too, have become the foundation upon which informal educational programs have been developed in museums, zoos, community clubs, summer camps, and many other settings.

All this research has been tremendously helpful in providing educators with the tools to reach and teach. What it means is that people with learning differences, including kids with autism, really *can* learn, assuming that material is presented in a manner that makes sense to the learner. And kids with autism really can show what they've learned, assuming that the educators are open to a variety of communication styles. If a child with autism can show his understanding, even nonverbally, an educator can respond with more and more challenging content. ·

But it's rare indeed for a child with autism to receive this type of instruction in the school setting. Private Montessori and Waldorf schools are loath to accept children with autism because they feel ill-equipped to manage what could be significant behavioral or social issues. Specialized "autism schools" exist to provide students with intensive therapies, with the goal of remediating challenges and supporting socially appropriate behaviors and language skills—not to find ways to build on kids' strengths and abilities. And just paying for such a school, even if it's your choice, can be a gargantuan task.

In the long run, therefore, the vast majority of children with autism are in traditional public schools, where academic instruction relies most heavily on precisely those "intelligences" in which autistic children are weakest—that is, verbal and social intelligence.

Too much talk

Teachers talk all day long, and they talk quickly. When they're not talking, they're asking students to talk or read. Students are expected to "grab" verbal information rapidly, translate its meaning, and respond appropriately, all within seconds. Students with autism are almost certain to be slower at verbal processing, both as listeners and as speakers, than are typically developing children. As a result, they may miss a great deal of what's being said or perform poorly when called upon to speak or write.

During the hours when students are not actually in class, they're engaged in open-ended social interactions. Lunch, recess, and transitions between classes are loud, unpredictable, and, for many children, stressful. Children with autism often find these chaotic periods unbearable. As a result, they may "act out," retreat, or otherwise behave in ways that make them stand out as problem students.

When students with autism do poorly in typical settings, they often wind up in separate "special" or "autism-support" classes where they receive intensive lessons in how to act and think more like an idealized version of other children. That is, they're taught (as much as is humanly possible) to be calm, focused, polite, engaged, and verbally responsive. In most American schools, they also receive support in speech, handwriting, and social skills with the goal of—someday—being reintegrated with their typically developing peers. All this, not surprisingly, is very hard work and can easily take up the majority of the school day. That means that there's really no time left over for pursuits that don't involve building verbal and social skills.

This goal isn't idiosyncratic: in the United States, it's the law. The Individuals with Disabilities Education Act (IDEA) requires that children with special needs receive a free and appropriate education in the "least restrictive setting." Today's interpretation of those terms generally means that students with autism are placed as often as possible in typical classrooms (sometimes with an aide), where they may or may not progress well personally or academically. If they are placed in a more restrictive (specialized) setting, the purpose of their education is largely to prepare them for reintegration into the general school population.

To meet the legal requirements of the IDEA, students with autism must be taught to learn in predetermined ways: verbally and socially. Teachers in autism-support rooms work hard to "scaffold" their students to the point where they can use verbal skills in a more typical manner. And children in the autism-support classroom (or similar setting) receive social-skills training. Like everything else in their school lives, the purpose of social-skills training is to help children with autism learn to behave more like everyone else. Through a variety of means, they practice play skills, physical skills, conversational skills, managing emotions, and generally getting along with others. In many cases, in fact, kids with autism are held to a higher standard than general education students who may or may not participate in discussions, make eye contact, ask and answer questions, and so forth. Sometimes social-skills coaching involves time with typical peers; just as often, it doesn't.

No choices, no exploration, no fun

Overall, students with autism have a very limited school life. Based on research that suggests children with autism need a great deal of structure, their days are often regimented. Based on the evidence that behavioral therapy (ABA) works, many spend the majority of their days responding to commands. While structure and therapy are obviously important, the enormous emphasis on these elements in an autistic child's education means that these kids are essentially outsiders to the actual school community. Rarely do they take part in after-school clubs, athletics, or even band. Our son, in fourth grade, was the first child with autism ever to take part in the school band— and now, in seventh grade, he remains the only child with autism the band director has ever included in her jazz program (he may well also be the only homeschooled child, too, but that's a different story).

School officials don't think twice about scheduling therapy sessions during music class or social-skills training during art class. Often, when same-age peers are off visiting the museum or the zoo, children with autism are on field trips of their own, practicing "life skills" by ordering at McDonald's or selecting fruit at the grocery store. After all, the thinking goes, these kids don't need music, art, or exploration: they need to know how to manage ordinary daily tasks.

By placing "typicalness" as the single most important goal for children with autism, the educational system overlooks the reality that these children really do learn differently. By focusing a huge percentage of the schools' time, money, energy, and ingenuity on teaching children with autism to be just like everyone else, the schools—and often parents and therapists as well—wind up neglecting the abilities, passions, and possibilities that almost every autistic child has in abundance.

This neglect is not intentional. Everyone has the child's best interests in mind, but the intense focus on remediation means that children with autism have virtually no opportunity to explore the wide world, experience the possibilities available, or find their own areas of strength, interest, or ability. As a result, they're unlikely to connect with like-minded individuals, build relationships based on common interests, or find opportunities to learn, grow, and lead in fields that interest them.

The time is right to get out, explore, and have fun with your child

Today, with rates of autism diagnosis at 1 in 100 (and even higher for young boys), autism awareness is big business, and kids with autism-spectrum disorders seem to be a part of every family. Whether or not the actual number of people with autism has risen, the number of children with autism diagnoses has gone through the roof. Today, most people know a child with an autism-spectrum diagnosis, and it's probably fair to say that just about everyone in North America, at least, knows or has a child with a related or similar disorder (Tourettes, ADD/ADHD, nonverbal learning disorder, OCD, etc.).

Community organizations are getting the message that families living with autism may want opportunities for their children—and themselves—outside the therapeutic setting. With interest in and awareness of autism so high, many organizations are working to include kids on the spectrum. Museums, camps, sports organizations, and community groups are all realizing that the family with an autistic child is a valuable commodity. You have concrete needs, and you're willing to travel and/or pay to get those needs filled. And as a community, you're connected: once a family with autism has a good experience, the members spread the news. In this economy, as families are cutting back on their community involvement, your family means a lot.

Meanwhile, media attention that is focused on negative treatment of kids and families with autism is helping to raise awareness and increase tolerance. From churches and synagogues to airlines, movie theaters, and bowling alleys, managers are becoming more aware of kids with special needs. No one needs the negative publicity that can quickly spread through the Internet when a coach, Scout leader, teacher, church, or entire neighborhood mistreats a child with autism. And everyone, today, needs the extra nickels that they can make when families with autism spread the word about a positive experience.

When kids with autism get out into the real world, they find people, places, programs, activities, and interests they'd never have experienced in the closed box of therapies and schools. Sometimes, those interests grow into volunteer opportunities or internships— in some cases, careers and relationships can result. Perhaps even more important, parents and siblings desperately need the sense of community that they are denied when children with autism are part of the family. Anxiety, depression, stress, and health issues can result.

With all these reasons to get out and get involved, why don't kids and families with autism get out into the wide world? Let's examine a few possibilities.

IGNORANCE OR ANXIETY ON THE PART OF PROGRAM PROVIDERS

There are certainly plenty of summer camps, sports leagues, and even churches that flat out refuse to include kids with autism in their organizations—even when they claim to have a mission of inclusion. The reasons are usually based in ignorance and/or anxiety: what little they know about autism is very scary, and they're afraid that your child will either cause a serious problem or drive away their existing clients/members. It's not easy to get past this roadblock, though some pioneering families have made great strides by either shadowing their children (thus, providing an easy way to manage any problems that arise) or by advocating on behalf of the autism community. For many families, the experience of being turned away from a community program just once can be traumatic. Better not to try, some families feel, than to experience that kind of rejection.

PARENTS BELIEVE THEIR AUTISTIC CHILD SHOULD BE IN THERAPY DURING EVERY SPARE MOMENT

Given the media frenzy around autism and therapy, many parents feel overwhelmed by a sense that they should fill every moment with some form of therapy. Many of the therapies available recommend as many as 40 hours a week of intensive one-to-one work, and while some schools provide this, many don't. Meanwhile, families may be trying multiple types of therapy all at once, thus eating up even more time. How can we do anything other than therapy with our child, parents wonder, when there isn't an extra hour in the day to go anywhere or do anything?

PARENTS ARE AFRAID OF FAILURE OR EMBARRASSMENT

Every parent hopes for a child who will make him proud. And it's true that kids with autism may embarrass their parents by strange or problematic behaviors. They may be the worst player on a team or have a meltdown in the middle of an event.

ADULTS HAVE LOW EXPECTATIONS OF CHILDREN WITH AUTISM

How could a child who's unable to make a single friend be successful as a band member? Create a work of art? Earn a black belt? In fact, the ability to make friends or manage a typical school setting may be completely irrelevant to success "outside the box." You don't need to say a single word to play the clarinet like a pro. Artistic talent often goes along with social awkwardness. And martial arts, while they require interaction, are predictable and rule-based: there's no guesswork or small talk required.

PARENTS ARE PROTECTIVE OF THEIR CHILD WITH AUTISM

Children with autism often act younger than their age. Most are easy to tease and bully. And many have experienced the pain of being the odd person out in a school situation. As a result, parents may decide to keep their child safe at home, or at the very most, they might involve their autistic child in "special" programs where she will be protected from bullies and supported even when she's unable to perform well. Of course, there are situations in which parental protection is a very good thing, and no one would advocate pushing a child who's unprepared into a situation that's too difficult. But by keeping a child with autism from pushing the envelope of her abilities and comfort zone, parents may stunt the child's growth. No one can develop a sense of self-esteem or earn the respect of others if she's never challenged to exceed her own limits.

PARENTS ARE UNAWARE THAT MULTISENSORY LEARNING MAY BE IDEAL FOR THEIR CHILD

Schools tend to focus on autistic children's deficits. Individualized Education Programs (IEPs) are written to remediate challenges, and, of course, kids with autism are continually challenged in the school setting. Often, teachers, therapists, and parents unwittingly mistake challenges in school for disabilities across the board. If you've never taken your child to the zoo, you have no way to know whether he'll enjoy and learn from the experience. And if your focus is entirely on building "typical" skills and remediating deficits, you may never find out.

CHILDREN WITH AUTISM MAY ALSO BE UNINTERESTED IN THE MOST COMMON KIDS' ACTIVITIES

One of the challenges of "out-of-the-box" thinking for some parents is the reality that kids with autism may honestly dislike ordinary pastimes such as sports leagues, birthday parties, or play dates. That might mean that the parents themselves must step out of their own comfort zone to explore, for example, model train clubs, Lego Mindstorm competitions, Manga conventions, or other venues where their child can shine. If your child with autism can live outside his comfort zone all day long at school, it seems reasonable that parents can take a few hours a week to explore their child's areas of special interest!

FAMILIES AND TEACHERS ARE UNAWARE OF THE RESOURCES AVAILABLE

Often, families are aware of only the best-publicized options for their children with autism. That is, they know of Easter Seals, Variety Club, and the Special Olympics. But they may not know that, for example, most YMCAs offer adaptive swim at no extra cost—and that their instructors are glad to accept kids on the spectrum into almost every program they run. Parents may not be aware that the Boy Scouts offer special training to Scout leaders to prepare them to work with autistic boys or that some museums offer special accommodations just for the benefit of families with autism. That's what this book is all about!

The bottom line: Getting out and exploring may be easier than you think

A few years ago, it was tough to include a child with autism in the ordinary activities of life. Misunderstandings about the nature of autism, combined with embarrassment, anxiety, and other issues meant that families had the choice of staying home, taking advantage of limited special-needs programs, or facing down judgmental neighbors. Now, the possibilities for kids and families living with autism are far broader, and parents and teachers, armed with information and ideas, can help their children and themselves to step out into the wide world. It takes work and patience, but the opportunities available are surprisingly vast.

It's also possible that a child with autism may make his parents proud indeed. Only by getting out into the wide world can a parent see his child overcome an obstacle and rise to a challenge such as running the bases, performing on stage, or winning a merit badge. And only by allowing a child with autism to experience the world can a parent discover a child's unexpected talent in art, music, science, or athletics.

Besides—and this is very important—the fact that a child is "typically developing" does not mean he will be capable, kind, attentive, or self-aware. In other words, you needn't assume that your child's autism will make him more difficult or less competent than other children.

Only last week, I watched as a typically developing six-year-old—who knows why?—walked down the bowling alley and climbed in among the pins. When the resetting machine suddenly plunked down on his head and the gate came down in front of him, he panicked—and nearly destroyed the entire mechanism struggling to get out. What was his mom doing all this time? Watching, with a half-smile on her face. Would your child with autism do something like that? If the answer is "probably not," or "I wouldn't let him," you're ahead of the game!

Pay attention, too, to the behaviors of typically developing children your child's age. How well do they comply with adult rules of social interaction? While your autistic child's teachers and therapists may expect your child to make eye contact, say hello, ask appropriate questions, respond with appropriate answers and so forth, typical children are under no such obligation. As a result, plenty of ordinary, typically developing children ignore greetings (or wave a hand while attending to a handheld video game), avoid eye contact at all cost, rudely push or shove others in line, and otherwise behave, well... like children. Your child's behavior may look eccentric (she may flap while a typical child might bite his nails), but the reality may be that your child is nowhere near as different as you imagine her to be!

Meanwhile, getting out and exploring the world can change your lives and the lives of your typically developing children for the better. If you have typically developing children as well as a child or children with autism, you've experienced the reality that only by getting out and about can you meet other families, find congenial groups and activities, and become a part of the community. If you have only a child or children with autism, you may be very busy but also very isolated.

As you start to get out and about with your autistic child and begin to discover areas where your child's abilities, passion, or personality shine, you too will start to meet other parents and get involved. You'll meet other parents for whom ordering the band T-shirts is a very big deal—and for whom trips to the therapist, IEP meetings, and other autism-related activities are nonexistent. You'll probably find this experience both fun and refreshing: an opportunity to experience life in the "real world" with your child.

You may even discover that your child's "perseverations" or "obsessions" with anything from trains to superheroes to football to theater will change your life. You may, for example, start to share your child's interest in model-train layouts, comic-book collecting, or knowing all the players' stats. Not only will your relationship with your child change, but you yourself will find whole new directions to explore, people to meet, and opportunities to expand your horizons.

This is a good thing. Yes, it's great for your child. But it's also great for you and for your whole family.

Top tips on why getting out, exploring, and having fun matters

- Think about your expectations for your child with autism. Are they limiting?

- Think about the types of activities that your child with autism enjoys. Keep in mind that these may not be the most common activities available for children.

- Begin looking into community activities that will allow your child to build on his real strengths and interests.

- As you look around, ask yourself whether your child could grow with this activity, or whether it will only be relevant for a short time. An amazing array of activities do have the potential to provide a lifetime of learning, growth, fun, community, and opportunity.

- Consider the possibility that you might enjoy the experience of getting involved in community programs with your child on the autism spectrum.

- Give yourself—and your child—permission to take a few hours a week "off" from therapies and school.

Chapter 2

Before You Start

Preparing Yourself and Your Child to Get Out, Explore, and Have Fun

Can your child learn to play a musical instrument? Become a long distance runner? Build a robot?

There's really no way to know for sure unless your child has the opportunity to try.

For kids with autism, finding out may take many tries, lots of experimentation, and some real dedication on the part of parents, community leaders, and peers. But in the long run, it's very possible that your child with autism or Asperger syndrome will discover places, people, and activities that bring out his talents and inspire his joy in living.

Why take the time to involve your child in real-world pursuits?

In today's world, we're told that kids on the autism spectrum should be receiving therapeutic support as early and as often as possible—with breaks only for meals, bathroom, and sleep. The idea is that, with enough intensive therapy, your child will "defeat" autism and become "indistinguishable from his peers." Schools focus diligently on remediating your child's deficits but rarely see fit to mention or build on his abilities. And so it seems clear that there simply isn't enough time in the day effectively to address your child's challenges and also build on his strengths.

If you think about it, though, it's a heck of a challenge for a child who lives 24/7 with one-on-one therapies, doctor visits, social-skills groups, and special diets to become "indistinguishable from his peers." By segregating your child with autism from ordinary activities and pursuits, you make it nearly impossible for him to identify with or even understand what other kids are up to or talking about.

A child who has never been exposed to ordinary "kid culture" is at a disadvantage—period. In the United States, certain brands, television shows, and activities define "kid culture." A kid who has never watched *SpongeBob SquarePants* on Nickelodeon (a kid-oriented cable television channel) will certainly get confused when the conversation turns to the characters in the popular show. And a kid who doesn't know how to use a swing properly is going to have a heck of a tough time fitting in during recess. For a child with autism, being clued in is even more critical than it is for a typically developing child.

And a child who has never taken part in ordinary kid activities (even to the point of knowing what they look like) will certainly never be able to take part in those activities typically. Whether it's collecting trading cards, building with Lego, fishing, bowling, swimming, or just playing on playground equipment, kids with autism need more exposure—not less. Picture yourself walking into a room full of strangers all of whom seem to share a knowledge of and interest in something you've never heard of. How easy would it be to break into the group or the conversation? For your child with autism, the task is simply overwhelming.

By involving your child—and yourself, by extension—in the ordinary world, you make it possible for him to know what's expected of him, not just by therapists, parents, and teachers but also by peers. What's more, you make it possible for him to discover his real world likes and dislikes, abilities and weaknesses, friends and allies. And you make it possible for you, as a parent, to enjoy those abilities and pleasures with him.

Another problem with the therapy-and-school-only model is that it places your child in a permanently artificial, supported situation. How can anyone become truly friendly with children who are only talking to her because a therapist requires it? How can anyone learn to play a musical instrument when her only experience with music is in a therapy session? And how can a young person build relationships based on mutual interests when she's never offered the opportunity to discover or share her real passions? It's also very, very tough to know what your child can really do when she's constantly supported by professionals whose job it is to ensure her success (or at least her lack of failure).

Naturally, therapy is important for a child with autism. But your child is still the same little person whom you imagined hitting a baseball, winning a prize, or otherwise excelling in life. As you work to provide him with the help he needs, bear in mind that he's still a child (or a teen). And, like all children, he's loaded with potential and possibilities.

Risk-free explorations to try with your child

Many parents of children with autism choose to stay away from public situations for excellent reasons. They don't believe their autistic child really will be able to take part in community-based activities—either because she won't comprehend what's going on or because she will behave inappropriately, or both. They may also choose to avoid distractions from therapies that they feel are more important than any outside pursuit might be.

If you've never seen your child take part in ordinary activities in a situation that's conducive to her success, though, you can't know what she loves, what she could do, or how far she could go. Your child may not be showing her talents, interests and abilities because no one has ever offered her the opportunity to do so under circumstances that are comfortable and inviting. And school is rarely an ideal setting for any child, let alone a child with autism.

A child who is never invited to sing outside a school setting, for example, will never know whether he enjoys or is good at it. Many children with autism are excellent singers—and a surprising number have the unusual gift of perfect pitch. Your child may not be able or willing to sing in a group of 24 peers, as directed by a harried music teacher in a room full of stimulating posters, instruments, and general clutter. But he may find it easier in a small chorus in a simple, uncluttered practice room.

Similarly, a child whose entire experience with physical activity consists of occupational- and physical-therapy sessions may have no idea that she enjoys dancing, swimming, diving, or tumbling. The fact that your child does poorly in gym class may be completely irrelevant to her actual talents, abilities, and interests. After all, gym class is really all about loud yelling, complex rules that are verbally communicated, and expectations that are rarely obvious. Ballet, gymnastics, karate, and a whole raft of other physical activities, though, are conducted in quiet spaces, with small groups and clear, repetitive rules.

So what will your child love? What will she hate? Where should you go first?

If the answer isn't obvious (your child is clamoring for karate lessons, for example), or you're very concerned about getting out into public spaces with an autistic child, I suggest you conduct a few simple "experiments" in your own home, backyard, or local park. The great thing about experimenting at home or in a private setting, of course, is that you can see for yourself what works and what doesn't—without risking an emotionally draining meltdown or embarrassment. What you'll discover is that your child, whether verbal or nonverbal, talented or not-so-talented, is a person with real preferences and abilities. You may be surprised to see what your child really does know, can do, and enjoys.

Here are a few points to consider as you get started.

THERE'S A FINE LINE BETWEEN INTEREST AND PERSEVERATION

If your child seems interested in a particular activity (or seems to have a talent), that's terrific. But kids with autism can get "stuck" on favorite characters, actions, locations, and so forth. When that happens, your child may not be engaging with the experience but simply repeating it for comfort's sake. As a parent, you will probably be able to tell the difference. For example, your child may love Elmo and, thus, find it great fun to "meet" Elmo at a theme park. But then again, he may perseverate on finding Elmo to the point where he can't engage with any other aspect of the park. This, obviously, is less than ideal—though it's a starting place. By experimenting at home, you'll find areas of interest that your child can enjoy and also grow with.

KIDS WITH AUTISM MAY DO THINGS DIFFERENTLY

You may envision your child immediately grasping the rules of a game, interacting appropriately with other kids, or behaving typically in a public setting. Chances are, though, your child won't cooperate with your vision. Early on, for example, we thought it would be important (and socially useful) to teach our son to play typical board games. We were delighted when he appeared to love the game Mouse Trap—but we quickly realized he was interested only because he enjoyed setting up the complex Rube Goldberg device that makes up the central focus of the game. He had no interest in actually *playing* the game. That told us that he wasn't quite ready for board games—but he *was* ready to build contraptions and sculptures, to visit the local science museum where a fabulous contraption had been installed, and so forth.

CONVERSATION ISN'T ALWAYS KEY

At school, verbal interaction is terribly important. In many other settings, though, it's less of an issue. Typical boys, in particular, talk a whole lot less than their teachers think they should or than parents believe they do (spend a little time watching a group of boys and count their verbal interactions!). In many settings, a "hi" and "good-bye" suffice—and in other settings, no words are needed. In short, don't allow your child's lack of verbal skills to place too many limits on your options.

YOU MAY NEED A THICK SKIN

Your child is autistic. That may mean he has extraordinary talents of which you can be extraordinarily proud. But it also means that your child will behave differently and may occasionally do things that you find embarrassing. Once you decide to get out and into the community, you'll need to be okay with that occasional embarrassment. That may mean growing a thick skin—thick enough to avoid reacting when some clueless adult or kid gives your child a dirty look for pacing, flicking, or putting his hands over his ears. To enjoy outings with your child, you'll need to decide that it's okay for your child to be himself.

HAVE FUN

While the activities in this book are "for" your child with autism, they're also for you. They're intended to offer parents and siblings the tools to get out there and have fun *with* their autistic family member—or at the very least, to provide you with a sense of connection to community organizations that you may have felt were out of reach. Try your best to find activities that you can enjoy with your child (or, ideally, with the whole family). If her choices aren't yours (she loves hiking, and you prefer arts and crafts), give hiking a chance. Who knows?—maybe you'll find a new way to get out, explore, and have fun.

THINK LONG TERM

As much as possible, think first of activities that have the potential to be of lifelong interest to your child. In that way, you'll provide him with the tools he needs to be involved with the community forever. If possible, start your child out doing something that will provide him with real, meaningful skills and tools. What that might mean is choosing violin lessons over "Fun with Music" classes, choosing baseball over T-ball, or choosing a bicycle over a scooter. "Just for Fun" classes, T-ball, and scooters are great, but in the long run you may find it hard for your child to transition to the real thing. Why not start with the real thing right off the bat?

Bear in mind that organizations like Boy and Girl Scouts, 4-H, and the YMCA do, in fact, involve children, teens, and adults: your child need not quit the organization simply because she has reached a certain age. In fact, all those organizations and hundreds of others offer volunteer, intern, and career opportunities for individuals with experience and passion.

Try it #1: Popular culture 101

Our kids are often sponges; they can learn almost anything by heart if it's introduced through videos, television, or even music. At first, we were horrified by our son's echolalia: he'd simply memorize entire scripts from his favorite TV shows and recite them. Later, though, we came to embrace certain shows and videos because they provided him with the tools he needed to engage with other kids, with the real world, and even with academics.

Like many parents, when our kids were small, we allowed only "educational television." But typical kids watch an awful lot of shows on advert-heavy cable TV. We didn't want either of our kids getting seduced by ads; but even more particularly, we didn't want our son wandering around reciting ads for breakfast cereals. So we started borrowing videos and DVDs of kids' shows from our library. We could choose our time to watch together—and avoid the ads completely.

If you have an autistic child who is mesmerized by television, you may have decided to turn it off permanently. Or perhaps you tend to use TV as an opportunity to get away for a much-needed break. Instead of flipping off the tube or walking away, try this:

- Choose a television show that your child really likes, and purchase a few toys (action figures, die-cast figures, etc.) that relate to the show. Don't worry if your child is "too old" for the show: plenty of grown-ups still love the Muppets, and even grandparents love Disney!

- Choose a time to watch together, and talk about the show as you watch. Ask your child questions; if he doesn't reply instantly, try saying outrageous things that he knows are wrong (for example, Big Bird is purple with green stripes, isn't he?). Your child's connection with and love of the show and characters may well prompt him to interact with you in new ways.

- Once the show is over, try using your new toys as puppets, acting out bits from the show. Or use them in interactive play (Thomas the Tank Engine is ideal for this since model-train layouts are fabulous tools for sharing, creative thinking, and role play). Let Thomas "talk" to your child, or have "Elmo" ask him questions.

- You may find that your child is more verbally responsive to Thomas the Tank Engine or Elmo than he is to other human beings—or more fascinated by the tracks than by the people playing with them. If that's the case, you can build on that in the real world! Your child might love attending puppet shows or going to TV-show-oriented events (a Wiggles concert could be an ideal introduction to concerts and plays, even if your child is "too old" for the Wiggles).

See Chapter 8, "The Visual and Performing Arts," for more ideas along these lines.

A note about Thomas the Tank Engine: for reasons yet to be explained fully, kids with autism are almost universally crazy about Thomas. This may sound like a problem, but it's a terrific opportunity because train museums around the world have embraced Thomas—and going to the museum to take an actual ride on Thomas may be an ideal way to start visiting museums in general. In addition, Thomas trains are based on real-world engines that can be found in museums and even on tracks around the world. Of course, kids who love Thomas may also love train spotting, visiting model-train layouts, and even building model trains. We've visited model-train exhibits at public gardens and museums, ridden trains in and out of major cities, gone to train museums and more—all because our son just loves Thomas the Tank Engine.

Not only have these experiences been great for Tom, but they've also given us a whole new area of interest that would never have occurred to us if our son wasn't crazy about Thomas the Tank Engine. In fact, along with Tom, my husband has now discovered the history of the Cape Cod railroad, ridden the Bay Colony Energy Train, located and photographed defunct and active train stations throughout the area, and even provided photographs for train-related exhibitions. Who would have guessed that all this could come from an autistic child's passion for Thomas Tank Engine?

See Chapter 6 on visiting museums and Chapter 10 on special-interest clubs for more ideas.

Try it #2: Out and about in the natural world

When your child is diagnosed with autism, you go into "fix it" mode. No more leisurely afternoons in the park for you and your child: it's more important to find therapies and therapists, visit doctors, follow up on therapists' recommendations, attend school meetings, and generally remediate your child's symptoms. Meanwhile, of course, there's still work, cooking, cleaning, your other children, your spouse, and an occasional haircut to consider.

With so much on your plate, it can be hard to find the time or inclination to take your child with autism on a simple walk in the woods, a visit to a pond, or a trip to the beach. Yet people with autism are often very much attracted to and connected with the natural world. And because there are few social or physical demands made by chirping birds, rippling brooks, or cool, green forests, you may find that your child calms down, relaxes, and enjoys himself. You may just find that you do the same.

To conduct this experiment, choose a nearby destination that is likely to be uncrowded and undemanding. Before you go, take a trip on your own with a camera or video camera in hand, and create a preview of your plan. Ideally, choose a location with a water attraction: a pond, lake, brook, river, or beach. People in general—and kids with autism in particular—seem to love water.

- Choose a day that's not physically challenging (terribly hot, cold, or wet), and tell your child about your plan. Show her your preview images or video, and discuss how long you'll be out (no more than a couple of hours), what you'll see and do, what snacks you'll bring along, what you might see along the way, and so forth. Then, get out and start enjoying.

- Pay close attention to your child's demeanor, her likes and dislikes, and her preferences. Does she enjoy walking briskly for long distances or get tired easily? Is she bothered by bugs or oblivious to them? Is the woods a good choice, or would your child be happier in a meadow, a city park, or another type of natural setting?

- What does your child notice? Our son happens to be very interested in birds and can spend a good deal of time watching birds on ponds, in marshes, and near harbors. To make the experience more interesting and fun for all of us (his parents, sister, and family friends), we now go for nature walks and bring along binoculars, a camera, and a field guide to birds of New England.

- If there is water in your area, spend some time there. Try skipping stones, or experimenting together by tossing in different types of objects (stones, pinecones, acorns, or wood chips). Is your child following your lead? Can you follow hers?

Once you have a sense of your child's comfort level in the natural world, you can start to relax and enjoy yourselves. If your autistic child finds the outdoors a comfortable place to be, try exploring Chapter 9 on camps and the natural world for more ideas for exploring, enjoying, and learning about the natural world together.

Try it #3: Musical instruments

When my son was in third grade, he learned to play a few recognizable pieces on the clarinet, and I thought it would be fun to bring the instrument into school and let him play for his autism-support class. He did, and the group applauded. Then the boys in the group asked if they could try, too. If you've ever tried playing the clarinet, you'll know it's not an intuitive instrument: it can be tricky to get anything other than a squeak out of it. Amazingly, to me, every child in the room was able to play the clarinet—right off the bat.

One boy was able, intuitively, to pick out a tune. Again, this is not a piano; it's a woodwind with a complex set of valves. When his mom came to pick him up at school, I told her about her son's ability and offered to put her in touch with Tom's clarinet teacher. She never called. To my mind, this was a terrible shame. Not every kid is going to love the clarinet; however, many kids with autism are not only musical but have exceptional musical abilities.

- To find out if your child has more than a passing interest in playing a musical instrument, you'll have to offer him the chance to play. By far, the most intuitive instrument to offer a child is the piano (or, alternatively, an electronic keyboard or xylophone). The keys are easy to access, and it's not difficult to pick out a tune or a scale.

- If you can, sit your child down at a piano and play a familiar tune. Ask him to copy you. If he can, you'll know that he has an "ear"—as well as a desire to play. Let him fool around with the keyboard; you may notice that he starts to pick out scales or tunes. Since many people with autism have perfect pitch and wonderful musical recall, he may find that playing the piano is both engrossing and fun. (Note: While a real piano is a terrific teaching tool, there are many ways to offer your child exposure to music-making. Possibilities include electronic keyboards, children's xylophones (if you can, buy two!), and even percussion instruments such as drums and rhythm sticks. If you're not musically inclined, you can try playing scales, beating out rhythms, or picking out tunes.)

- If your child likes the piano (or any other instrument you've tried), consider exposing him to music of various kinds. It's not unusual for kids with autism to enjoy classical music, though many like different styles and genres. Consider the possibility of borrowing instruments from friends or teachers. Does your child enjoy drums? Horns? Strings? Does he enjoy dancing to music, playing music, playing together? We were amazed to find that our son, at a very young age, was able to sit through and enjoy the children's concerts at the Kimmel Center in Philadelphia, something our typical daughter found deadly dull.

- Pick up musical recordings and musical videos. We were amazed and delighted to find that movies like *Fantasia* and *Fantasia 2000* had a very powerful and positive impact on Tom and his appreciation for classical music. Audio and video recordings of *Peter and the Wolf* were similarly powerful for him.

- If it looks like your child has a special interest in a particular instrument, it might be time to consider lessons. Kids with autism have been known to thrive with the Suzuki method, though there are many other ways to learn. It took us a while, but we were able to find a young teacher who was neither a music therapist nor a special education therapist but who had the patience and creativity to work with our son.

For more ideas on making music a part of your child's life (and yours), explore Chapter 8 on the visual and performing arts.

Try it #4: Marble maze

Because kids with autism are often struggling with basic verbal and social skills, it's unlikely that most have had significant exposure to science (which, sadly, is often sidelined as a not-as-important academic field). Science, math, and autism, however, are often linked. In fact, some people think that Albert Einstein was autistic! Science can be much more than an academic discipline, too. It can be a door into a whole world of experiences, opportunities, and friendships.

Is your child with autism interested in physics? One way to find out is to introduce him to the marble maze. The marble maze is much more than just a toy; it's also a tool for learning about and experimenting with prediction, invention, physics, engineering, and even social communication. Marble mazes are often found in science and children's museums because they're not only fun and engaging, but they also teach basic physics.

Can your child with autism build, enjoy, and understand the purpose of a marble maze? To find out, you'll need a marble maze (Discovery Toys makes a good, solid, easy-to-build version, and there are many others on the market). You'll also need a few marbles.

Sara Cook, age 10, experiments with a transparent marble maze

- Start by building a very simple marble run. Ideally, you'll include a ramp and a spinner. Show your child how to release the marble and watch it drop through the run. If she seems interested, you can work with her to improve on the run: add one piece yourself, and hand one to her to add to the run. Alternatively, you can model construction of a run piece by piece, and have your child copy you.

- As you build, you and your child can experiment with marbles to see whether your maze works and where the ball will go. You can try larger and smaller marbles, lots of marbles, and metal ball bearings to see what happens. You can also add additional pieces to the maze: some kits have funnels; others have chimes, buzzers, spinners, and other engaging bits and pieces to add to the marble run.

- If your child enjoys the basic marble run, you can take your fun to the next level. Collect cardboard tubes and build a large-scale marble maze using duct tape and ping-pong balls. Drop different types of balls from a height to see what happens to them. Create a catapult out of a yardstick and a can, and launch your ball to see who can make it fly the farthest.

- Once you know that your child gets a kick out of building, designing, engineering, experimenting, or even just rolling balls, you have a great place to start. Your child might enjoy all kinds of related activities, including Lego building clubs, science-museum workshops, sand castle construction, or an after-school science club.

For more ideas related to science, engineering, and technology, explore Chapter 6 on museums and Chapter 10 on outings, clubs, and other ideas.

Try it #5: Sports and physical activity

When you have a child with autism, you may assume that he won't be interested in sports. That may be because of early, negative experiences on the playground, in group-oriented sports programs for young children, or in gym. But sports and physical activity can happen anywhere—and they can happen in groups or individually, as a family or as a pair. We've had very good luck with swimming, bowling, hiking, and now even biking, even though our son is not intrinsically interested in or good at typical children's games and sports.

- If your child is like many kids with autism, she enjoys chase-and-tickle games. These are very simple, rule-free interactions that involve an adult's playfully grabbing and tickling a little one. Chase-and-tickle games have the advantage of requiring almost nothing from the child except gleeful giggles, and they also offer kids the kind of sensory input that they may crave. If you've never played chase and tickle with your autistic child, give it a try. If she enjoys the interaction, you've made a great start. Chase games are very popular among young children, and chasing can be the start of activities such as relay races, which are, of course, a part of the repertoire of a track-and-field athlete.

- Your child with autism may also enjoy ball play but have a tough time managing the complex rules of ball-based sports. To find out if that's the case, just grab a ball and roll it back and forth with your child, bounce it, or practice "making baskets" with a trashcan. If your child shows an interest, try visiting a local playground or gym on off hours, and just play around together.

Nat Batchelder shoots some hoops

- You may find that your child has a good eye for getting the ball in the basket but can't really master the team play involved with the sport of basketball. If that's the case, there are many gyms (think of a YMCA or recreation center) where parents and children are welcome just to come and shoot baskets. Over time, your child may develop more and more of the nonverbal communication skills needed for team play, and when that time comes, he'll be ready with the basic ball-handling skills to play the game. Meanwhile, you'll have improved your parent–child bond, given your child great experience with physical exercise and hand-eye coordination, and also included him in a community activity that can be of interest for his whole life.

- If you find that your child has a knack for or interest in a particular ball-based sport (soccer, basketball, football, baseball, cricket, etc.), you have a great starting place for getting involved with spectator sports, too. You can watch games at home on the television, invite a few friends, and then build up to attending a local game. With enough preparation, your child might even enjoy attending a game at a big stadium.

- Another sport to experiment with is swimming. Kids with autism often enjoy water, and swimming may come very naturally. The great thing about swimming is that it's very versatile. It's easy to swim as a family, but it's also possible to swim as part of a team in a pool, lake, or ocean, with other kids or on your own. However, if you're taking your child to a pool and she's not yet potty trained, she will need to wear a special swim diaper (available in most drug stores in the U.S.). Of course, potty training isn't as critical in ponds or the ocean, but you still may not want to deal with a mess. Start off in the shallow part where it is relatively easy: in the kiddy pool or in a pool where she can easily stand. Make as few demands as possible;

just enjoy floating around and having fun together. If your child shows an interest, you can consider lessons or provide lessons yourself. Of course, it's very important that your child build enough water skills to stay afloat, but excellent stroke skills and the ability to dive aren't critically important. If your child is really interested in going further with swimming, individual or group lessons may be in order. And if your child turns out to be a great swimmer, swim teams are a terrific option.

See Chapter 4 on sports and Chapter 8 on the visual and performing arts for more ideas and resources.

More quick, easy ideas for getting involved

Kids with autism don't always have or show interest in typical "kid" activities. But no matter what your child's interests or abilities, there's always a way to build on them in the real world.

One parent wondered how she could possibly build on her daughter's fascination (actually an obsession) with dragons. As it turns out, dragons are a terrific entrée into a whole world of social activities. You may not ever have visited a renaissance fair, for example, but for a dragon-loving child, it's like heaven on earth. Dragons are also, of course, the centerpiece for all kinds of video and role-playing games (hence, the name of the game Dungeons and Dragons). They're also the focus of artistic and cultural expressions around the world and can be found in most major art museums, at celebrations of Chinese New Year, at amusement parks—in short, dragons are everywhere.

If it's possible to build on dragons, imagine what you can do with your child's existing passion for the following.

ANIMALS

Visit a pet store, a zoo, an aquarium, or a farm. Volunteer to help at an animal shelter or nature center. Attend a "live animal show" at a local nature center or science museum. Go for a walk in the woods and find as many live animals as you can. Go birding or fishing.

TRAINS

Take rides on real trains, and allow your child to hand over the tickets to the conductor. Visit train museums, model-train layouts, and train yards. Join a model-train club. Build your own model-train layout. Go train spotting. Take a trip that involves a ride on a tourist-oriented train (narrow-gauge trains, trains in amusement parks, etc.)

LEGO AND OTHER BUILDING TOYS

Build a city together. Join a Lego or Lego Mindstorms club. Play Lego-based video games together, or invite others to join in. Use Lego-based software to create animations, and share them. Volunteer to create an after-school engineering and design club, and recruit your child as a helper.

Give your child a running start

As the parent of a child with autism, you know your child is not going to be able just to jump in and get involved with many community activities. No matter what her diagnosis on the autism spectrum, she will need preparation, accommodations, and support to make any inclusive activity work well. What's more, she may or may not be ready right away for community inclusion. As a parent, though, you're well equipped to prepare your child to get involved when and as she's ready.

Preparing your child can mean several things. It can mean literally putting together social storybooks, videos, or other tools to give him a clear vision of what to expect. This is actually very easy to do. To start, you may want to take a look at Carol Gray's *Social Stories*™ or the *Model-Me Kids*® videos: these are professionally created tools intended to prepare autistic kids for particular situations. Once you have an idea of what kind of preparatory material you want to create, all you need is photos, illustrations, or icons to include in a booklet that you share with your child.

Preparation can also mean practicing interactions, skills, or experiences that are likely to be a part of community-based programs or events. One parent planning a camping trip had her child practice sleeping in a sleeping bag, then sleeping out back in a tent. Other parents may want to practice "typical" activities such as circle time or saying hello. This type of preparation is especially useful in a situation where the agenda is set in stone: a religious service, a Scout meeting, or a concert, for example.

Yet another type of preparation involves building skills. Long before we enrolled our son in the school band, he had mastered the basics of playing the clarinet. As a result, the actual musical challenges of band were nothing to Tom, so he was able to focus on managing the social and sensory challenges of being part of an ensemble. The same principle applies to sports, clubs, and many other types of community activities. If your child is already solidly competent when it comes to kicking, dribbling, and passing a soccer ball, he can focus much more readily on the social and communications challenges of the game. Other kids and coaches will see him as an asset to the team. And, through the process of building skills together, you will have created a wonderful parent–child (or sibling) bond.

The least you need to know about getting out and exploring with your child on the autism spectrum

Throughout this book, you'll find tips and suggestions that relate to specific types of community activities and groups. Over and over again, though, you'll find iterations of the same basic suggestions. If, after looking at these basic suggestions, you feel energized and excited, you'll have a terrific time getting out there (even if you're tired but inspired). If, on the other hand, these basics seem overwhelming, you'll need to take things slowly. Bear in mind that even one excursion, one new experience, one new interest pursued is 100 percent more than most families try.

- Know that the process of finding the right program, activity, or group for your child with autism will require some research, some experimentation, and some false steps. The right settings are out there, but they may not be the nearest or most obvious choice.

- People with autism need preparation before they try something new. It's up to you to be sure you have what you need to help your child get ready and feel comfortable in a new setting, coping with new rules, and meeting new people.

- Know that, sometimes, your child will need to take baby steps forward. Instead of regretting your decision to leave the house, it's important to celebrate the fact that your child took part—even just for a little while—in something new. Key to succeeding in this is to avoid spending a great deal of money and time on a single event or excursion unless you're absolutely certain your child can handle it.

- Be aware that kids with autism can get overwhelmed or upset for reasons that are not obvious to others. Whatever the reasons for an unexpected meltdown, it's absolutely critical that you always have an alternate plan "B" to put in place—a way to calm things down gracefully and comfortably or even decide it's time to call it a day. That way, you're never defeated: you're simply taking things a step at a time.

- Take it easy on yourself and your child. Kids with autism may well exceed your expectations, but they may never look just like everyone else. If they don't, it's okay: they're behaving like themselves. Rather than comparing yourself and your child to the star athlete, singer, or Eagle Scout, give yourself and your kid a break: you're here, you're part of the process, and that's a long, long way from where you started!

- Remember that the point of getting out, exploring, and having fun is to get out, explore, and have fun. If that's what you're doing, you've succeeded! If your child is also building skills and making friends (or if you are), it's all gravy.

Tools you'll need to get out and explore with your child

Take a deep breath. Let it out slowly. Remember that this is a process. While some outings, events, and programs will be absolutely smooth as glass, some won't. Before you get out there, be sure you have these tools.

AN INTACT SENSE OF HUMOR

For some parents of kids with special needs, having a sense of humor is no joke (pun intended). If you are the kind of parent who grimly does daily battle to secure every available treatment or service for her child and calls a lawyer at the slightest sign of a glitch, you may find yourself quite overwhelmed and unhappy with community programs. The reality is that, unlike schools and social-service agencies, these organizations are not familiar with autism, they're not set up to provide accommodation, and when they say "yes" to your child, they're taking a step into the unknown. Give them, yourself, and your child a little breathing room—and when something crazy happens, take it with a smile.

TIME

Parents of kids with autism are often racing from meeting to appointment to meeting. But getting out into the community means taking some time to smell the roses, and it also may mean taking time to check out and experiment in a lot of settings, some of which may be a good distance from your home. If you're going to be stressing every minute that you're out fishing or cheering your child's bowling league or sitting in on a Scout meeting, the experience will be negative for you, your child, and any community leader who gets between you and your schedule. Of course, you can take inclusion one step at a time, and the best solution is to take on no more than you can comfortably or easily handle. After all, this is supposed to be fun!

ENERGY

Parenting takes energy. Parenting a child with autism takes extra energy. Parenting a child with autism outside the protective box of special-needs programs and classes may take even more energy. If you're exhausted, it won't be fun for anyone. Again, take it a step at a time—there's no need to overwhelm yourself.

GASOLINE

Unless you're incredibly lucky, you won't find perfect matches for your autistic child in programs located right around the corner. We drive well over an hour to our son's fabulous math tutor, and it's well worth it—but with the cost of gas constantly rising, it's not a cheap choice.

PATIENCE AND FLEXIBILITY

It's going to take some time for you and your child to find the right community activities and program. It's going to take some time for community leaders really to "get" your child. It's going to take some time for your child to start feeling at home and thriving in the community. You may need to try more than one option before you settle on something that works really well. There may be setbacks or frustrations along the way. All those things, though, are predictable: you can plan for them. What you can't plan for is that moment when your child, for the first time, shows what he can really do—and it's just breathtaking.

Ready to step out

Once you've determined your child's interests, tried different activities in a private setting, prepared your child, and prepared yourself, you're ready to head out into the community. Each chapter in this book provides specific ideas, information, resources, and cautions to consider, so you can step out with confidence.

Remember that kids with autism need patience and creativity to succeed. That means that you, the parent, will need to practice deep breathing, develop a thick skin, and have a number of different ideas and options to share and try. If you're wondering whether it's worth it, the answer is clear. Not only is it important for your child to get out there into the community, but it's essential for you, your partner, and anyone else who's intimately involved with raising your child on the autism spectrum.

Remember, too, that your child will grow and develop. He may need a whole lot of support on Day One, but by the time he's been involved with a group, a sport, an organization, or an activity for a year, he may be far more capable than you ever imagined. One of the keys to success, of course, is allowing your child to try, make mistakes, and even fail as he learns to participate in the "real world."

About siblings of the child with autism

There are many excellent books, websites, and resources available to support the siblings of a child with autism. None, however, can take away the complex and sometimes painful emotions associated with having a sibling with special needs. As you think about and prepare to bring your child with autism into the public eye, it's important to remember that your typically developing children are likely to have concerns. Those concerns can range from the practical (*Am I supposed to look out for him at the fair?*) to the ethical (*Is it okay to have a play date and leave my autistic brother out of the play?*).

There are also more self-centered questions to address: *Why is my brother with autism allowed to get up during dinner, but I'm not? How come Mom spends so much time with my autistic sister and not me? If we go out together as a family, will my autistic brother embarrass me? What if my sister flaps her hands or makes her weird noises in front of my friends?*

As you start to get out into the world with your whole family—including your autistic child—you'll need to think about and plan for these types of questions, which are legitimate and reasonable. I recommend setting clear limits to your typical child's responsibilities for a sibling with autism, while also making it clear that the autistic child is a respected and beloved member of the family. For example, when we send our two children to day-camp together, we do ask our daughter to keep an eye out for Tom—and occasionally, she "translates" for him when others don't quite understand his intent. But we also make it clear to everyone (including Sara!) that Sara is *not* Tom's aide and that any significant questions or concerns about his abilities or behavior should be addressed to us, not to her.

I also suggest, as possible, that you make the limits clear to your autistic child and that you ask your child with autism to keep his siblings' concerns in mind. While a person with autism can't control his feelings or suddenly gain social skills, most people with autism can choose to follow specific, carefully selected social rules in specific situations. And, as possible, it's reasonable to set down those rules and expect them to be followed. For example, Tom enjoys reciting stories to himself in the car—a form of self-calming that's perfectly acceptable most of the time. But when our daughter's friends are in the car, we ask him not to recite or laugh to himself—and he's quite capable of holding off until the friend is dropped off at her home. This makes for a much more positive sibling relationship and less of a feeling on Sara's part that having her brother around creates embarrassing problems.

In our family, we also work hard to be sure that our typically developing daughter gets plenty of parent–child time, with and without her brother. That's made a whole lot easier by the fact that we are homeschooling Tom while Sara's at school—providing us with plenty of "Tommy time" during the day. When Sara comes home, we're then much freer to attend her soccer games, help with homework, and go with her to events and activities that are important to her. Of course, not every family can homeschool. But the principle remains the same, as it does for every family: each child is unique, and each needs and deserves at least some special parent–child time.

Top tips for preparing yourself and your child

- Go easy on yourself and your child. Community inclusion isn't a race; it's a process that will continue throughout your life.

- Be flexible and creative in your community choices. Maybe your child with autism hates soccer—but who knows? He could become a world-champion fencer!

- Know that not every setting will work out well, and be prepared to decide it's the wrong match or the wrong time. Consider trying a more promising setting at a later time.

- Be aware that both your child and the community leader will need preparation, support, and even a little hand-holding.

- Take advantage of existing resources such as videos, websites, social stories, and other tools to prepare your child and your community leader.

- Be aware that typically developing siblings have their own very real needs and concerns that should be addressed.

- Do your best to allow your child with autism to be challenged, to try, and even to fail. Only if she actually overcomes challenges and obstacles can she earn the respect of herself and others.

Chapter 3

How to Learn About and Select Community Settings for Your Child and Family

The choice of the best setting for your child with autism isn't always obvious.

When Tom was little, he showed an interest in music. He enjoyed plinking the piano keys and seemed to have a natural ability to pick out scales and chords. At preschool, he had a fabulous experience with a visiting music therapist. And so we decided that it would be fun to try an interactive music class.

To be sure the experience would be positive, we asked the preschool who had provided the program that Tom had so enjoyed. We learned that there was a multisession music program for young children starting in just a week at this facility. There would be a different instructor, but the activities would be similar. No one was concerned that Tom had special needs, especially since one of his parents would be there each week (every class member came with a mom or dad).

We started the class with high hopes. It was held in a big mansion that had been converted into a music academy. There were only about ten kids in the class, and the whole program was geared to experimentation with rhythms and instruments. How perfect!

But soon after we arrived, it became clear that Tom was not going to be paying much attention to the instructor. Unlike the instructor who'd visited his preschool, this very kind, gentle lady wasn't able to hold our son's attention. She asked the kids to sit and listen, and only after ten or fifteen minutes were they asked to participate. By then, we'd already run after and retrieved Tom three or four times (he wanted to check out the instruments—*now!*).

After the third session, we decided the class was not going to work for us, and we quit. We never did go back to those delightful preschool music classes, since they clearly weren't right for Tom.

When he turned seven, though, Tom decided he wanted to play "the horn," and a friend presented us with a clarinet. Interestingly, it was the same homey music academy we'd left several years before that was able to provide us with an instructor willing to work with our son. We wound up coming back to the academy every week for more than three years (after which our wonderful instructor moved to a different setting, and we went with her).

The moral of the story: no matter how careful you are about choosing a community program, there's no way to know ahead of time whether the match will be right. But just because your child isn't ready for a particular experience today doesn't mean he'll never be ready. Tenacity and flexibility are the keys to success.

Tommy Cook plays clarinet in the middle-school jazz band (2009)

Exploring your options (yes, you have options!)

Today, the YMCA, Boy and Girl Scouts, museums, and an incredible range of community and private programs are very aware of the huge rise in kids with "special needs." Fewer and fewer program directors are likely to say, "We can't help you" when you mention a developmental delay or even an autism diagnosis. And more community groups than you'd expect have actually gone out of their way to learn about and provide supports for kids with autism, ADHD, and similar developmental differences.

The problem is that too few parents, teachers, therapists, and support groups are aware of how things have changed—not only for our kids with special needs but for families overall. There's much more openness to special needs families, if for no other reason than the fact that we now make up some 15 percent of the family market overall. And it's also much more acceptable than ever before for parents to take an active role in their child's informal learning experiences. Parents hang out and take part in arts programs; they attend every athletic practice; they camp out along with their young Boy and Girl Scouts; they attend every meeting of YMCA Adventure Guides. As the parent of a child on the autism spectrum, who needs you by his side, you're not as unusual as you may feel.

It's not always easy, though, to find the right match for any individual child with autism. The fact that a program is "open to" kids with autism doesn't mean it does a good job of reaching and engaging any particular child. Not every child with autism will thrive in a drama club, a baseball league, or a Sunday school class. But when you find that good match, it's truly magical—not only for the autistic child but also for the community leader who has learned that he can connect, engage with, and coach a child who really, truly needs him.

Your role in your child's success

It's not only the child with autism who benefits from true inclusion: it's the whole family. Parents and siblings find that they can, at last, feel that they're a real and legitimate part of a community. Your child with autism may find himself becoming a truly valued member of a cast, a team, or a club—and you may find yourself taking an active role in the ordinary parenting chores of carpooling, painting sets, selling cookies, or clapping at the end of a performance. All these things can happen. All it takes are huge quantities of energy, time, tenacity, flexibility, tact, communication, patience, and—sometimes—gasoline.

Sound exhausting? Supporting your child with autism as he builds competence, self-esteem, and real relationships in the community can take a lot, but bear in mind that (unlike trips to the therapist) it can be fun, energizing, and exciting. Imagine applauding your child as he performs on stage, earns a merit badge, or kicks a ball toward the goal. Imagine joining other parents as they set out the juice and cookies and sharing your good feelings. These dreams are not out of reach, even if your child is nonverbal or profoundly delayed.

One key to success is finding the right setting, activity, and people who can value your child for his abilities, rather than pity him for his challenges. A second and equally critical key to success is *you*.

In addition to searching out the right settings for your child and providing the support she needs, you'll also have to manage your feelings of discomfort or embarrassment at seeing your child look or behave differently from her peers. This is no small challenge: we parents are "programmed" to look around for judgmental expressions and to become defensive when we feel our child is undervalued or questioned. But it's natural for other children and even for other parents to have questions about your child if she moves, speaks, or behaves in surprising or different ways. You'll need to decide how to manage your own feelings under those circumstances. Along with the community leader who's working with your child, you may or may not want to address the issue head on with a "lesson" on what autism is, what it isn't, and how it specifically affects your child.

And at the same time, you'll need to find it in yourself to step away as your child begins to find her own way. This can be very hard, especially when there are obstacles for her to face and overcome. She may have to work harder than the average child to win a badge, prepare for a recital, or move up to the next level in tumbling, dance, or karate. Of course, as a parent, you'll help her to achieve those goals. But if you make the process too easy (Janey wins a prize every time, no matter what her performance), then your child loses out on the opportunity to strive and succeed in her own right. What's more, the people around your child begin to see her not as a member of a group but as a "special case" whose achievements are less significant than those of their own children.

When your child with autism succeeds in a real-world situation, it should be a cause for real celebration. To allow that to happen, you'll need to allow your child to take responsibility as much as he possibly can for his own self-care and self-management. You'll need to step back and allow him to make mistakes or even fail (assuming that he's receiving enough support actually to be able to succeed with effort). It may take two or three tries to pass the swim test, earn the merit badge, or win the race. But as is the case for everyone, autistic or not, if there's no challenge, there's no sense of accomplishment, no shared sense of pride, and no acceptance by the group of a person who took on the challenge and succeeded.

Styles of community inclusion

There are, in essence, four ways to include a child or teen with an autism-spectrum disorder in community activities. Each may be appropriate for your child in different settings, or at different points in his life or yours.

The *first option* is to take advantage of special-needs programs, which are often developed as offshoots of typical programs. Little League, for example, offers its "Challenger League" program. Variety Club and Easter Seals both offer full-scale summer camps strictly for kids with disabilities. There are many other such programs available, some through general community agencies and others through private and/or nonprofit organizations. For some kids with autism and for some parents, this is a safe, appropriate choice. For Tom, special-needs programs were a helpful starting place, though in the long run, we've found that he can find both acceptance and respect within certain "typical" community programs. Sometimes a child with autism needs the extra support of a "special" program in athletics but can be included without any support at all in another situation.

The *second option* is to find a semi-inclusive program. Generally, this is a program for typical kids that will provide an aide or at least welcome an aide or shadow to support your child. If the program doesn't provide a support person and you, personally, can't be present, it's often possible to hire or, through various programs, gain access to a one-on-one aide. We've done all these: we've sent Tom to semi-inclusive programs, we've hired aides to support Tom in typical activities, and we've provided one-on-one support ourselves in typical classes when the instructor seemed willing to include our son but unsure how best to instruct him. We've found that, on occasion, being available to provide direction and support to a young or anxious instructor or counselor was very helpful. Not only did our son benefit from having one of us on hand, but also the leader, instructor, or counselor learned a great deal from us. Leaders learned how to work with our son, and at the same time, they also learned that *autism* isn't a dirty word and that working with a child with special needs can be a fun, positive experience. Often, as I've worked on this book, I've heard program providers express their sense of fulfillment when they discover that they really do have what it takes to help a special child exceed expectations.

The *third possibility* is to create the programs and/or run them yourself, thus ensuring that your child with autism has a friendly, supportive program leader and that all aspects of the program are appropriate for your child. Parents of kids on the spectrum often run their own Cub Scout packs, 4-H clubs, and so forth. This can be a very effective approach, though the parent leading the program will need a great deal of energy to provide support not only for his own child with autism but also for other children in the program. In the long run, though, this approach may place you, the parent, in an awkward position. What if your child is the only one who doesn't "get" or enjoy an activity? What if your child needs to leave the room or needs extra help? In such a case, it's critical to have the support of other adults.

The *fourth option* is to find the right typical setting for your child with autism, cross your fingers, and walk away. This may seem like an impossibility, and it's true that many settings (and leaders) will be all wrong for your child. But there really are many adults out there who can reach, teach, engage, and care for your child with autism, sometimes helping him to exceed even your hopes and dreams. These adults are not therapists: they're instructors, counselors, coaches, and community leaders who just happen to click with your youngster. This book focuses most on such opportunities—with the important understanding that choosing the right settings (and walking away when they're wrong) is the key to helping your child develop relationships, skills, and opportunities.

First steps

You've made the decision to step out with your autistic child. Now what? As you start thinking about the options, there are a few rules of thumb to consider.

START SMALL

Parents overall seem anxious to load their kids up with extracurricular activities, but for the child with autism, just one new experience can be more than enough. Similarly, parents often want to see their children thrive in the company of lots of kids; perhaps it's because the sight of our child in the company of others gives us the sense that they're cultivating friendships. In fact, though, large groups can easily be overwhelming to kids with autism. Small, structured groups are often a good way to get started.

START WITH AN ACCEPTING LEADER AND/OR ORGANIZATION

Parents of kids on the spectrum may feel that their child should be included in any setting and that it's up to the program provider to figure out how to make inclusion work. In fact, though, not every coach, instructor, or community leader is capable of providing a positive experience to a child with special needs. If someone tells you she can't provide a good experience for your child, take her remarks at face value. It really doesn't matter whether the leader is snobbish, anxious, or simply incompetent: if she doesn't want your child, there's no point in making an issue of it. Simply move on. Even if you decide, in the long run, to take legal action or otherwise press for inclusive practices, it's neither fair nor helpful to place your child with autism in an unwelcoming situation.

ACCEPT THAT THERE WILL BE GLITCHES

Even if your child with autism is doing well in a community setting, chances are that something will come up at some point that will require your involvement. That's okay: that's what parents are for. If you're prepared to step in as needed, you may be able to troubleshoot and get things back on track.

DON'T TAKE OFFENSE EASILY

Kids with autism can be confusing and frustrating. They may reject kindly meant gestures of friendship or become anxious and upset for no apparent reason. When that happens, you may hear negative things said about your child. If those things are true, there's no need to take offense. Rather, it may be much more helpful to step in and facilitate, provide some hints and tips, or allow your child some time away.

DON'T WORRY TOO MUCH ABOUT APPEARANCES

It's not easy to see your child running a race and coming in last. It can be painful to see younger children outdo your child at bowling or dance or art. In fact, embarrassment can be one of the toughest aspects of parenting a child with special needs. It may take your best acting ability to appear nonchalant when your child misses the ball for the third, fourth, or fifth time. But if you're obviously agitated, everyone around you will pick up on your cues—including your child, the group leader, and the other children.

KNOW THAT NOT EVERY SITUATION WILL WORK FOR YOUR CHILD

The program director may be wonderful. The program itself may be ideal. And yet your child may have a rotten experience for no obvious reason. Sometimes, these things happen, for every child. If everyone's doing his or her best and your child is still unhappy, the best choice may be to withdraw from the situation. You may well be able to come back to the same organization a couple of years from now and find that your child is ready to take part.

AVOID ACTIVITIES THAT REQUIRE HIGH LEVELS OF VERBAL AND NONVERBAL COMMUNICATION

Few kids with autism do well with nonverbal communication, and many do poorly with verbal communication as well. So it makes sense to avoid starting out with a typical team sport or program that relies heavily on great communication skills. This sounds obvious, but when every other kid is involved with soccer or hockey, it can be tough to hang back. It's important, though, to avoid setting your child—or yourself—up for failure.

MAKE CHOICES BASED ON YOUR CHILD'S INTERESTS, NOT YOURS

Don't choose a program based on your own personal goals or preferences. In other words, your love for music shouldn't be the basis on which you choose to include your child with autism in a music program. Similarly, your personal goal of "inclusion in typical sports" may or may not be realistic (or any fun) for your child.

AVOID HIGHLY COMPETITIVE SETTINGS

This is important for several reasons. First, highly competitive settings are likely to attract leaders and kids who will be less tolerant of your child's differences. Second, such settings are likely to attract parents who have even less tolerance for differences than the leaders and kids. Third, highly competitive settings are usually too fast moving for children with information-processing delays. There's no need for your child with autism to enroll in the dance class filled with kids who are heading for Broadway—a low-key, stress-less dance class is probably a better choice. (Of course, if your child turns out to be a wonderful dancer and decides he's Broadway-bound, a more intense program will almost certainly be just fine.)

Sara Cook, Paige Mead, Lisa Jo Rudy and Tom Cook explore hydroponic lettuces at the Coonamessett Farm in Falmouth, MA

SEEK OUT EXPERIENCED INSTRUCTORS

Try not to choose settings in which the leader is brand new to instructing children. While some very young, very new leaders can be quite talented, in general, experience counts when it comes to working with kids. Program leaders with experience under their belts know that all kids are unique, and they may well have worked with a child like yours.

Where to start looking for the right setting for your child

There's a saying: "If you know one child with autism, you know one child with autism." This saying is absolutely accurate. Kids with autism are as different from one another as they can be—with the one exception that all have problems at some level with social communication. Given that kids really are very different from one another, there's no simple way to guess which setting(s) might be best for your child.

A good way to start your search is by asking questions of other parents of kids on the spectrum. Which sports leagues, churches, camps, after-school programs, or museums have great reputations among the autism community in your area? At the very least, you'll find out which leaders and organizations are welcoming to kids with different learning styles and challenges. Be aware, though, that a program that works for a friend's child may not work for yours. The reasons for these differences may include basic interest (their kid loves soccer, your kid is an animal lover) or differences in functional level or sensory issues.

Our son, for example, has a marvelous time at aquariums, despite the fact that they're almost always crowded and noisy. That's because his sensory issues are relatively mild, and he's just bananas about marine animals. Most kids on the spectrum would also enjoy visiting the sharks, but only if their local aquarium offers a special time when kids with autism can enjoy the site in relative peace and quiet. Kids with Asperger syndrome may be capable of participating in activities like Boy Scouts or drama club, while children with more profound autism may find these activities to be overwhelming. Thus, while a recommendation from another family with an autistic child may be a good starting place, it's no guarantee of success.

If other families aren't able to provide an ideal recommendation, look around—all around. It's easy to assume that your child will do just fine in the local Cub Scout pack or after-school program. But the fact that a program is convenient doesn't mean that it will be right for your child. You may need to travel to find the right match for your child with autism, and you may need to experiment. It's okay to pop into a museum for a short visit or to "audit" a club or activity. If you're told that your visit is not welcome, that's probably a good sign that the organization is not going to be flexible or accommodating enough to provide your child with a good experience.

As you start digging into options for your child, there are some specific tips to bear in mind.

START WITH YOUR CHILD'S INTERESTS

There may a good, local soccer league in your town; but if your child doesn't understand, enjoy, or want to play soccer, there's no reason to get him involved. In fact, if your child feels that an inclusive experience is a form of punishment, he's likely to act accordingly. Instead, look for programs that reflect his active interests. If he loves trains, you might want to think about a visit to a local model-train layout. If he enjoys sports but needs extra support, you might need to travel to find a really appropriate program.

THINK OUTSIDE THE BOX

It's true that most typical kids enjoy sports, but your child isn't typical. What might he enjoy out in the wide world? It's quite possible that your child with autism will have a terrific time at an art gallery. Or he may get a huge thrill out of singing in public. Or he may be a natural at fishing. There's absolutely no reason why your child with autism has to conform to the "usual" pastimes of his typical peers.

ASK QUESTIONS

Actually, if you're not sure that a program or setting will be right for your child, ask *a lot* of questions. What's the adult-to-child ratio? What would the instructor do if a child isn't following instructions or is having a tough time doing what's asked? How involved can you be as a parent?

ASK MORE QUESTIONS

Who knew that parents of Cub Scouts are encouraged to attend camp with their kids? That many YMCAs have adaptive swim lessons available free of extra charge? That many museums partner with local autism groups to train staff to adapt programs and even support autistic volunteers? The only way to find these things out (outside of reading this book) is to ask. The answers may surprise you.

VISIT

A program director can be the greatest guy in the world, but he's not the one with whom your child will be interacting. In fact, the director may be a great fundraiser but have very little idea of what life is like "in the trenches." That's why it's important to visit—both with and without your child—to get a true sense of the program or experience you have in mind.

DESCRIBE YOUR CHILD'S NEEDS

You may or may not decide to use the word *autism*, but it is important to let program leaders know that your child has special needs. Some parents describe their children as "developmentally delayed;" others mention specific issues (*my child may have a hard time warming up to peers; my child may need extra help with fine motor tasks;* etc.). You'll know right away if there's an issue: body language and tone of voice will make it obvious if your child is not welcome.

CONSIDER A TRIAL RUN

Anyone who is familiar with the autism spectrum knows how incredibly different kids with autism can be. One child on the spectrum may have a wonderful time at a science club, for example, while another may be unable to manage the fine-motor or communication demands. A smart, experienced program director may not immediately say "yes" to your child until he has had a chance to meet her. If a leader is unsure as to whether your child will do well in his program, it might be wise to suggest a site visit or trial period.

Why would a community organization want my child to participate in its programs?

As you explore this book more fully, you'll find information on a wide range of community activities, events, and venues. You may start to wonder whether, in fact, all these venues are really as accepting as I suggest.

Of course, the answer is that every venue will be different. But as a fundraising professional (among my many hats), I can tell you that there are good reasons for nonprofit institutions to include children and families with disabilities in their programs. Those reasons are not wholly altruistic. While most nonprofit educational, athletic, and religious institutions do mention "inclusion" somewhere in their mission statements, it's only recently that they've actively engaged with and even sought out families with disabled children. Here's a few reasons why.

WE ARE NOW A LARGE ENOUGH DEMOGRAPHIC THAT IGNORING US IS FOOLHARDY

In this day and age, nonprofits and even private clubs need every member they can drum up. If some of those members have autistic kids, institutions are finding that now is a great time to find a way to accommodate those kids.

THERE'S FUNDING FOR INCLUSION

Most nonprofits rely on grants to at least some degree for their daily bread. Grants that could once be considered "gimmes" are now highly competitive. Autism is a major cause, and many foundations (federal, state, and private) are interested in supporting programs that support kids with autism.

MEMBERS AND FUNDERS LOVE A GOOD STORY

And the success of a child with autism as a result of an organization's dedication is a terrific story. By presenting their success with kids on the spectrum, institutions can solicit positive media attention and develop really compelling annual appeals.

SPECIAL-NEEDS FAMILIES SPREAD THE WORD

We are on the Internet, attending meetings, and generally connecting more than the average parent. As a result, programs that work quickly receive attention. Camps, classes and organizations can become popular overnight when they receive positive press from the autism community.

What all this means is that you, as the parent of a child with autism, are in a privileged position. While it may take extra work to find the right setting and support for your child, you can do so knowing that your involvement is a plus for the institution of your choice. If you so choose, you and your family can help your local institution through a variety of means. Details about just how to help with fundraising and public relations are included in the final chapter of this book.

Should we discuss or reveal our child's autism?

In many cases, there's simply no getting around the fact that your child is different. His idiosyncratic language (or lack of words), his physical demeanor or stimming, or his lack of social reciprocity may be self-evident. In that case, there's no question about revealing your child's diagnosis. The question, in that case, is what to say about it, whether to a community program leader or to the other children in the group.

Across the board, people I interviewed for this book (parents and community leaders) say communication is key. The more you can tell a group or program leader about your child's needs, challenges, and abilities, the better. Some organizations even ask parents to provide a school Individualized Education Program (IEP) because the school often lists accommodations that make learning and social engagement easier for your child. In theory, at least, your upfront work should ensure that the leader has the time and information she needs to include your child effectively. By the same token, if you don't say a word about your child's autism and then he shows up and is clearly disabled, it's reasonable for a group leader to feel pushed into a corner, unprepared, perhaps even angry.

It's quite possible that if you tell the leader ahead of time that your child is autistic (or has developmental delays), he or she will looked shocked, hem and haw, and finally say, "I'm really not sure we're prepared to provide your child with a positive experience." If this happens, in my experience, you should take the statement at face value and walk away. Clearly, the leader is not ready, able, or willing to find creative accommodations for a child with any kind of difference—so why go there?

But what happens if your child's autism is not self-evident? Many children with high-functioning forms of autism and Asperger syndrome do not display overt signs of a disability. They may walk, talk, and move very much like a typical child. Then, something comes up—a missed social cue, a sensory assault, or a series of frustrations—and your child falls apart in ways that are very different from the ways his peers react. An example of this is the twelve-year-old boy with Asperger syndrome who is having a fine time playing dodge ball until he's actually hit by the ball and told he's "out." Instead of just sitting down (according to the rules)—or even angrily denying he was hit, as can sometime happen with typical children—he bursts into tears and runs away. This is an atypical response for a twelve-year-old boy, and it has the potential to be embarrassing for the child, confusing for the other children, and upsetting for the leader.

If your child is something like the twelve-year-old in the example above, it's very important indeed to prepare the leader. But depending on your situation, your child, and the institution and leader you're working with, you may or may not decide to use the word *autism*. The "A-word" can bring up a whole host of media images that are completely irrelevant to your child—and some organizations will even turn away children on the basis of a specific diagnosis because they don't fully understand the range of the autism spectrum (we've had that experience more than once). Instead, parents may opt to use the terms *developmental delay, young for his age, sensitive*, and so forth. No matter what word or phrase you use, though, the important point is to let the leader know what to expect and, even more important, what to do about it. Should she leave your child alone? Give him a comfort object you provide in advance? Lay down the law? You're the expert on your child's needs—and in cases like this, it's up to you to share your expertise.

Top tips for community involvement

- There are four options for including your child in community activities. In order of least inclusive to most inclusive, they are: (1) special-needs programs; (2) semi-inclusive programs; (3) fully-inclusive programs in which a parent is very involved; (4) full unsupported inclusion.

- Start with a realistic vision of what your child can manage, and what your community organization can handle. Explore settings that seem likely to support not only your child's interests but also her special needs. Avoid settings that expect a high level of social communication.

- Think outside the "usual" box of kid-friendly activities. Your child might be a great match for unusual programs or sports—anything from junior ranger programs to fishing derbies to robotics clubs.

- Experience the settings and activities for yourself before bringing your child along. Get a feel for the style of the leader, parents and kids. Are the expectations reasonable for your child? Is the group supportive? What happens if someone slips up or gets frustrated?

- Talk to the community leader who is most involved with the kids. Ask lots of questions, and not only listen to verbal responses but also observe their body language. Is this person truly welcoming of a child with autism, or just giving inclusion appropriate lip service?

- Visit with your child, and let him have a chance to try out the experience with no strings attached. If it isn't a good match, be prepared to say "thanks but no thanks."

- Know that you and your child are not asking for favors. You're asking to take part in a community program that's open to all. And as a part of a growing demographic, you have some financial clout.

Chapter 4

Sports and Autism

Sports and autism rarely seem to go together, and that's a shame. The reasons probably have something to do with the delayed gross-motor skills that often go along with autism-spectrum disorders. They also probably relate to the reality that gym and recess are appallingly challenging settings in which to learn to love physical activity. Or maybe it's because so often parents assume that children should be involved with team sports—an assumption that may place sports out of reach for kids on the autism spectrum.

The good news is that the world of sport is much broader than the gym, much more structured than recess, and much more varied than the games offered through school or even through local recreation departments. And even if your child with autism turns out to have no interest in participating in sports, there's always the world of spectator sports to consider. Your daughter may not be an athlete, but she may be an avid fan, scorekeeper, and team supporter!

If your child does find a true interest in a particular sport, nurture it. Consider the possibility of advocating for your older child or teen to be offered leadership opportunities. Perhaps your teen could be the assistant manager, the equipment wrangler, a demonstrator, or a scorekeeper. Bear in mind that every sport is a business, and every business needs passionate, knowledgeable professionals. If your child loves swimming, Tae Kwon Do, horseback riding, basketball, or hiking, there are worlds of internships, volunteer opportunities and jobs out there for people like him.

Beyond soccer

When soccer is king

If your community is soccer-obsessed, you may believe your child with autism has no place in the world of sports. If that's the case, think again. Soccer is a great sport, but it's just one among dozens of possible ways to get moving and having fun. The problem, of course, is that it may be tough to find those other options if you're living in a world of soccer moms, soccer kids, and soccer coaches.

In the United States—and in many other countries around the world—virtually every child older than three (and some even younger) learns to play soccer. While this has some logic in countries like the United Kingdom, it makes little sense in the United States, where few native-born Americans even bother to watch the world soccer championships—and very few adults play the game.

What makes it even stranger as a choice for young children is that soccer is a very complex game. It requires a whole slew of skills that are beyond the ability of most children under the ages of nine or ten. Sure, the average three-year-old can kick. But can he actually keep his attention on two sets of players and manage his movements such that he is available to receive a pass from a teammate and move the ball down the field—understanding the complex rules governing off-sides, fouls, and use of hands?

As any parent of a child in peewee soccer will tell you, the answer is no.

But with all these caveats, as families know, soccer is king. Soccer isn't just an activity, like dance class or tumbling. It's a major element of middle-class life. Not only do children participate in the sport, with the more athletic children covering their families in glory, but mothers often build friendships around soccer-related carpools and social events. Fathers build their relationships with their children around coaching, cheering, and practicing soccer skills.

What does all this have to do with autism? Children with autism have challenges in the areas of physical coordination, social communication, verbal understanding, and the ability to read nonverbal cues that make the game of soccer about as tough as any activity could possibly be. But soccer is king, and parents are anxious to see their children—and themselves—included in the "soccer club."

Because of this atmosphere, far too often kids with autism are "included" in soccer with no real attention to individual needs. As a result, they wind up standing uncertainly in the middle of a field or wandering aimlessly, while typical peers race around kicking, cheering, and scoring. For the child with autism, at best, the experience is neutral, neither pleasant nor unpleasant. At worst, the experience can be humiliating, upsetting, or confusing. For the parent of the child with autism, the outcomes are no better. And while it's possible for a child with autism to enter a "special" soccer club, the outcomes may not be much better. That's because soccer, like most team sports, is a game that builds on the very strengths that people with autism lack: verbal and nonverbal communication skills, social skills, and gross-motor coordination.

On beyond soccer

Actually, while soccer may, for uncertain reasons, be king among the elementary-school set, there are many, many other sports that are just as significant, just as well respected, and just as physically challenging as soccer. What often makes these sports a better choice for most kids with autism is that they build on the interests and abilities of the child, build self-confidence, fitness, and coordination—but require far fewer social and communication skills. As a result, kids with autism can not only succeed but also, at least sometimes, can also even excel.

Top sports for kids with autism

Assuming that you and your child have decided that typical team sports are not a terrific option, what are some of the best sports for kids with autism?

Of course, kids are kids, and they're hard to predict. Who would have thought that my son Tom would actually enjoy and excel at tennis, when just a few years ago he ran from balls headed his way? But there are some "best choices." Notice that most of these sports, unlike many of the more popular team sports, can become lifelong interests. This is important for people with autism, many of whom prize consistency and routine and for many of whom learning a new sport can be a major project. Here are some of the top options, based on the experiences of families and kids living with autism.

Swimming

Swimming is a wonderful sport for most people, including children with autism. Kids who have a tough time with ball-handling skills can very often do well with basic strokes and typical water play. Parents and kids with autism can and do have a great time swimming together—in pools, at the beach, in a pond, or even in a wading pool. What's more, there

Nat Batchelder swimming for the gold at the Special Olympics State Games

is no reason that a kid with autism who has solid swimming skills can't take part in a swim team, especially since swim-team members compete individually.

Getting started with swimming may involve a fair amount of trial and error, since kids with autism may have trouble with group lessons, water in the face or eyes, and other issues. There may also be concerns about potty training (swim diapers work well for kids up to ages five or six, but after that, it may be impossible to find a diaper that fits).

Assuming that your child with autism is either very young (and in a swim diaper) or potty trained, you might want to start swimming in the simplest way: just by splashing around together in a pool or pond. If you're successful in getting out and having fun by getting wet, you've made a terrific start—and you might want to stop right there.

If you decide to go further, you can investigate swimming lessons in your area. Many YMCAs have pools, and many Y pools employ trained aquatics experts who have experience with special-needs kids. In fact, many Ys today even offer "special swim" as a part of the regular schedule. If there's no YMCA in your area, there may be opportunities for swimming in summer at a municipal pool, year-round in a hotel or school gym, or in warm weather in a lake or pond.

Swimming has several important plusses that other sports don't. Among them:

- Swimming is a whole-body exercise that builds muscle, endurance, and lung capacity.

- Swimming is a well-established sport that allows for individual ability and preference. Whether your child is slow or fast, good at one stroke or another, or even prefers diving, there's a place for him on a swim team.

- Kids of all ages and all abilities can have fun together in the water with no reference to rules, physical strength, or even communication skills. Watch a group of teens at the beach, and you'll see as much roughhousing, chasing, and splashing as you'd see in a preschool wading pool!

- Families can enjoy water play and swimming while on vacation or in their own community. And they can do so with no fear of judgment. After all, everyone's kid splashes, few kids practice their perfect strokes just for fun, and plenty of typical kids have a fear of diving off a diving board.

One word of caution: deep water is dangerous. If you do plan to have your child around deep water, it's very important either to have her wear a life preserver or—ideally—to have solid enough swim skills that she can stay afloat.

Horseback riding

Horseback riding is an expensive endeavor. That aside, though, it's a terrific sport for kids with autism. In fact, many autistic kids ride horses as a therapeutic activity (as such, it's termed *hippotherapy*). It's not unusual for autistic kids to find it easier to communicate with animals than with people, and many autistic children excel at horsemanship.

Sarah Wiseman and her horse, Emmy, after a cold winter's ride on the beach

Horseback riding is one of those sports that can be enjoyed at many levels, from the simplest pony ride to the most impressive equestrian event. It's also a sport that offers opportunities beyond itself. That is, horsemanship is much more than just riding; it also can include grooming, learning to put on and care for saddle and bridle, mucking out the stables, and generally being responsible for another living creature.

Our initial experiences with horseback riding involved pony rides at a "special" summer camp. Our son loved the ponies and seemed to have a knack for sitting up properly in the saddle. On the basis of that experience, when he was a bit older, we signed him up for a week at a typical (tiny) day camp that offered pony rides and horse care every day. Even to this day, Tom talks about his "favorite horse" and remembers pony camp fondly.

Some children with autism start out in hippotherapy, riding horses to build both strength and communication skills. After some time in the therapeutic setting, they may "graduate" to real lessons—and thence to competition.

Nancy Wiseman, an author, entrepreneur, and autism mom, has a daughter who is far more involved with horsemanship than Tom was. The details of Nancy's journey into the equestrian world are discussed later in this chapter.

Track and field

Strangely, Americans teach their youngest children to play complex team sports like soccer while only high schoolers seem to compete in running and jumping! For kids with autism, track and field may be a terrific outlet. Track events require fewer nonverbal communication skills than most team sports, yet kids who excel at track are valued team members.

It may be hard to find a track-and-field program for young children in the United States, though it may be a bit easier in other countries. Fortunately, it's not hard to find places to practice the basic track-and-field skills of running and jumping. Just visit your local high school after school hours—or, in some communities, your local recreation area or park.

Nat Batchelder getting psyched to run the Best Buddies 5K Marathon

Running is a great activity to start with your child. It's simple and basic, it's good for both of you, and it can easily lead to involvement in community 5K runs, fun runs, running clubs, etc. It's also a great way to build a skill that's of critical importance in many other sports—soccer, field hockey, baseball, and so forth.

If your young child is really excited about track and field, it may be worth your while to consider starting up your own local track-and-field group for young children. You may be able to find support through the schools or your local recreation department—but since track requires relatively little in the way of equipment, you may be able to just do it on your own.

Bowling

Even though it's loud, bowling seems to be a natural sport to many kids with autism. Perhaps it's the repetition—bowl twice, sit down. Or maybe it's the satisfaction of seeing the pins come crashing down. Whatever the reasons, plenty of kids with autism not only enjoy but also are really good at bowling.

Bowling has a lot of advantages as a sport for kids with autism. Like many other sports, it can be played with family, with groups, on a team, or solo. It's a popular activity for birthday games, so knowing the basics means your child will be well prepared for a bowling party. Bowling can be played year-round, which means that if your child loves it, she can do it even in the dead of winter. Lastly, plenty of people bowl poorly and bowl anyway; if your child is among them, it's really no big deal.

Most bowling alleys have "off" hours when you and your child can bowl without worrying about crowds or lines. And many have low-cost times during the week when your child can spend as long as she likes without the activity's becoming a financial drain. Most bowling alleys also offer the option of "bumpers"—pull-down, rubber-lined boundaries that make it almost impossible for a ball to go into the gutter. If your child is easily frustrated, bumpers ensure success right off the bat.

We found that our son loved a sport called "candlepin bowling"—very similar to ordinary ten-pin bowling, but with smaller balls and thinner pins. The sport, offered only in New England, is a great way to get started. But Tom enjoys ordinary bowling, too.

We got Tom started in the local candlepin-bowling league because he simply enjoyed the sport. Early on, he used two hands to bowl, which in theory made him a standout (though we were told there was no rule against two-handed bowling!). After about a year and a fair amount of coaching, he graduated to one-handed bowling and very creditable scores.

We were thrilled, at the end of year one, to find that Tom's team of three boys had actually earned more points than any of the other teams (granted there were only three other teams, but still—very exciting). Tom was proud to be among the trophy winners. Even better, it turned out that Tom had improved his score more than any other kid in the league and earned a second trophy!

Hiking and fishing

For many people with autism, the peace and quiet of the natural world are great stress relievers. Hiking, which can be an individual or group activity, is an easy way to get exercise and enjoy nature without the pressure of intense social communication. And it's super-easy: just lace up your shoes, pick a destination, and go! We've found that our son, who has little interest in or energy for running, has an awful lot of stamina when it comes to multimile hikes in the woods. Depending on where you live, you might choose to ramble across fields, around town, or in lovely countryside. If you can, choose a destination that's not too far away but that holds some intrinsic interest—ideally, a watery spot (lake, pond, or stream).

Fishing is another sport that may be of interest to an autistic individual who enjoys the natural world. Typically, kids in general aren't big on holding the slimy worms or managing a flopping fish once it's caught; but if you, the grown up, can handle those "icky" chores, fishing may be a great sport to try.

Like any sport (but more so), hiking and fishing can graduate from short, local expeditions to overnight camping trips, weeklong rambles, and challenging climbs. You can join a hiking or fishing club, compete in fishing derbies, hike the Appalachian Trail.

Tom and Sara Cook fishing for crabs off the boardwalk in Sandwich, MA (2006)

Or you and your family can volunteer to clear or manage a trail, giving your whole family a purpose and direction that actually makes a difference.

Biking

Bike riding can be tough for kids with autism, since balance may not come naturally. Once the basic skills are mastered, though, cycling can be a wonderful way to enjoy the outdoors. Like most of the sports described above, cycling can be enjoyed alone or in a group, just for fun or in competition.

It took us a long time to get Tom on a bike. We tried starting with tricycles and training wheels; but as a very young child, he did not have the desire, the strength, or the coordination to get the bike moving. Later, we experimented with a "tagalong," an extension that attaches to the back of an adult bicycle and allows a child to pedal along behind. Tom enjoyed the tagalong but still felt nervous about trying a real bike on his own. And, honestly, while a tagalong is great for a five-year-old, it's less than ideal for an older child.

Soon, too big for the tagalong, Tom was on a tandem. Again, fun for him but quite a project for us.

Finally, this year, our town put in a fabulous bike path, and we determined to teach Tom the art of biking. Following expert instructions, we started him out on a small bike with the seat lowered and the pedals removed—just coasting down grassy hills. When he felt anxious, he could simply put his feet down to stop.

After six or seven sessions, he was confident enough to coast most of the way down the hill, and we put back the pedals. Slowly, he gained the confidence to pedal—and to stay balanced on the bike.

Nervous about getting out on the path with lots of other bikers, we then took Tom to the running track. There, he practiced pedaling on a "road," following curves and stopping when approaching a barrier. He's biking on his own and enjoying it.

Next summer, we hit the bike path!

Martial arts

While martial arts aren't sports in the typical sense, they are physical outlets. They also combine the elements of predictability and structure with the challenges of physical interaction with other people. For many kids with autism, the martial arts are a wonderful way to build physical skills along with self-esteem.

It is possible to find special-needs martial-arts classes, and if one is available in your area, you may want to check it out. Other options to get your child involved include private or semiprivate classes and parent-child classes.

A few other favorite sports of kids with autism

While I personally wouldn't have picked these sports out, they seem to be of great interest to many kids on the autism spectrum. This is impressive to me, since they require great stamina and balance. If your child has an interest in or talent for any of these sports, you may want to start with a "special" program to give her a head start.

- Skating (ice skating, including figure skating and in-line skating).

- Ice hockey.

- Skiing.

- Skate boarding.

- Dance (this is also a performing art but requires great athleticism).

- Yoga.

- Gymnastics.

- Trampoline.

- Golf.

Cubby Elder on skates at
Puffers Pond in Amhurst, MA

Getting started in nonteam sports

How do you get a child with autism started in nonteam sports? The answer is as individual as the child with autism—and his or her parents. Some children simply join parents or siblings in favorite activities; I know quite a few autistic children who have become impressive golfers, fishermen, and hikers simply because, like other children, they were introduced to the sports as little ones. In other cases, parents carefully select a sport based on some of the issues described in the last section. In yet other cases, much to the surprise of everyone, the child with autism chooses a sport himself and winds up enjoying it tremendously.

We were among those many parents who just assumed that our son—with or without autism—really should have the team-sports experience. After one or two abortive attempts at inclusion and soccer, however, we determined that teams and Tom were not a good match, and we moved on. Knowing that Tom, like so many children with autism, loved the water, we decided to try swim lessons.

Tom's first swim lessons at the YMCA were…a bit different. We signed him up at age three for the usual pollywog program. The Y instructors were happy to include him; but where other kids sat at the edge of the pool and attended to the instructor, Tom dipped his hair into the water and watched it drip, drip, drip into the pool. Nevertheless, he had no fear of water and seemed to do just as well as many typical children and better than some. We also noticed that Tom seemed to do best when taught by a young man with a brisk, upbeat style and that he tended to lose focus when taught by the many kind, gentle, female instructors who tended to baby him and allow him to slide by with poor strokes or half-hearted dives. Over time, swimming has been a regular and wonderful pastime for Tom and our whole family; it has opened doors for homeschool gym, family swim, summer camp, wonderful beach experiences, and more.

But while we were able to predict Tom's interest and ability in swimming, we've been very surprised by the sports he has taken up as an older boy. Tom's sister, a fearless athlete, developed a taste for rock climbing. With Tom's limited arm strength and discomfort with tight clothing, we thought a harness and belay rope would be a disaster. Much to my surprise, though, as we waited for sister Sara to take her turn at a climbing gym, Tom piped up, "I'd like to give it a try!" And so he did. While he'll never be a championship climber, it turns out that the fearlessness he exhibited in the deep end of the swimming pool stands him in excellent stead as he climbs 40 feet up a rock wall and then rappels down again.

Another big surprise for us was tennis. As a little one, Tom was so uncertain about the velocity and direction of balls that he'd literally run away rather than play catch. He was unable to throw a ball—period. Yet, at age 12, he actively decided he wanted to try tennis. We started him and his sister with semiprivate lessons, but he was then able to move quickly into a group program. Sara, our athlete, was actually mortified to find that Tom's strokes and accuracy are better than hers. And we learned that a two-handed forehand is a perfectly legal stroke!

Issues to consider when choosing a nonteam sport for (and with) your child with autism

If you're actively selecting a nonteam sport for (and/or with) your child with autism, you'll need to consider both her strengths and her challenges. Some sports require a high tolerance for heat, mud, and sweat. Others require balance, upper-body strength, or the ability to listen to and follow complex directions. Here are some guidelines to get you started.

WHAT DOES YOUR CHILD REALLY ENJOY?

If your child loves the water, swimming might be a great option. If your child is an animal lover, horseback riding could be a good choice (though stable smells may be overwhelming).

IS YOUR CHILD HIGH OR LOW ENERGY?

This varies tremendously within the autism spectrum. If your child is high energy, consider track and field (running, jumping) or physically demanding sports such as rock climbing (available at many YMCAs and in rock gyms across the U.S.). If your child is low energy, he might prefer bowling, hiking, or fishing.

DOES YOUR CHILD HAVE GOOD OR POOR PHYSICAL COORDINATION AND MUSCLE TONE?

Most children with autism have relatively poor physical coordination and muscle tone, but that can improve over time with the right choice of sport. Swimming, dancing, hiking, horseback riding, tumbling, martial arts, and biking are all sports that can start out very gently, allowing the individual child to build skills, strength, flexibility, and coordination over time.

DOES YOUR CHILD HATE TO LOSE?

If so, a sport that involves competition is likely to become frustrating. But there are plenty of activities that require no competition at all. Hiking, biking, yoga, dance, tumbling, fishing, golfing—it's amazing how few sports really require kids to compete on a team!

IS YOUR CHILD READY FOR INCLUSION IN A SMALL GROUP?

If so, some sports lend themselves to the "not-quite-ready-for-primetime" child with autism. Martial arts are fast becoming popular among kids on the spectrum, possibly because the interactions are formalized and predictable and the competitions are one-on-one. A more advanced youngster with autism might also find fencing or wrestling to be interesting for the same reasons.

IS YOUR CHILD WITH AUTISM INTERESTED IN INDIVIDUAL SPORTS ON A TEAM LEVEL?

Swimming, archery, track and field, bowling, fencing, wrestling, cycling, sailing, and many other sports allow children to be on and part of a team without the need to read others' nonverbal or verbal cues.

Skating and horseback riding: A success story

Nancy Wiseman is the mom of a daughter with autism and the creator of the nonprofit First Signs. Her daughter, Sarah, has taken up both figure skating and horseback riding and found both to be great outlets. Horseback riding may even turn into a vocation for Sarah, who can now be dropped off at the stables early in the day and work independently with the horses until late afternoon. Nancy says, "Working with horses is helping her independence and self-confidence and helping her to build a strong work ethic. She'd eventually like to run a horse farm and help kids with autism."

Here's how Nancy describes her daughter's experiences with skating and horsemanship:

> We started with a local skating program. I spoke with the director of the program and asked her if she had worked with any children with special needs. She said a few, but the important thing was she was very open and creative. She chose a coach who was best suited to Sarah. Although class sizes

were big, they were organized. She had difficulty staying up with the other children so I hired the coach to provide one-on-one lessons between group sessions. This helped Sarah to get up to speed quickly. She loved it so much we continued private lessons and she advanced a level every two months; faster than most kids. In two years, she passed 14 levels and started competing. She has placed first, second and third in a few competitions and, although she doesn't love competing, at least she tried it. She's now learning double jumps.

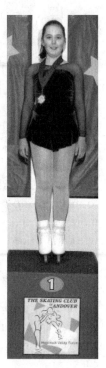

Horseback riding started a year and a half ago. That was entirely her idea. A couple of kids at the ice rink loved to ride, so we went to their instructor who had some experience with special needs children. It was fairly casual and the instructor was kind and gentle. Sarah loved riding so much she decided she wanted to ride more often and she wanted a trainer who would push her farther. Her new trainer uses a behavioral

Sarah Wiseman taking first place in a figure skating competition

approach—the opposite of what she's used to. Initially I was appalled that he would yell at the kids, but I realized it was for their safety—and Sarah needed to hear those safety messages. He's very strict and although this style has never worked for my daughter, she responded to it. She prefers the tougher approach because she wants to learn and compete, and her dream is to become an equestrian.

Team sports for kids with autism

Despite all the challenges and options described above, many parents feel that team sports are critically important to their children's physical and social development. Even though physical education may be incorporated into school programs, many schools are cutting back. Even more vulnerable are "adaptive" gym programs that address the unique needs of children with developmental and physical differences.

As a result, parents are looking for—and are willing to travel to—team sports programs that are right for their child with autism.

If you're hoping to get your child with autism involved with team sports, a good way to get started is by playing together just for fun. Whether you're shooting baskets, tossing the ball back and forth, or learning to skate, you'll be building both physical and social skills if you do it together. In the long run, it's experiences like shooting hoops with Dad (even when the hoop is lowered) that help build parent–child connections.

Special-needs or typical team sports?
Depending on the child, it may be possible simply to enroll in local recreation programs and anticipate success. It's usually easiest to do this when children are very young: few volunteer coaches expect three-, four- or five-year-olds to build serious athletic skills, and it's not unusual to have several team members lose focus as the ball heads toward their end of the field. But as children get older, both coaches and teammates expect physical, social, and communication skills that may be beyond the abilities of a tween or teen on the autism spectrum.

Should you look into Special Olympics, Easter Seals, or Challenger League options? These clubs have a great deal to offer in terms of support, adaptation, and spirit. It's important to remember, however, that they're not intended to teach skills or competition in the same way that typical teams do. So, a year in a special-needs sports program is unlikely to prepare your child with autism for a typical recreational league or school team. As Stan Jaskiewicz, a dedicated autism dad from the Philadelphia area, says, "Challenger is the exact opposite of inclusion." We'll hear more from Stan in a short while.

Finding special-needs team sports programs
Most communities of any size offer special-needs or adaptive sports programs of one sort or another. Many such programs are offered on an informal basis: a parent of a child with special needs decides whether a program is needed, and he or she creates it. It can be tricky to find out about such informal programs, but a great way to start is simply to ask around at support-group meetings, special-education

parent groups, and local area list serves. Occasionally, a gem of a program exists "under the radar," and membership grows strictly through word of mouth.

If you're interested in pursuing a more formal route to finding a special-needs team sports program, there are local, national, and international options available. In addition to those listed below, it's well worthwhile to research programs in your area; by "Googling," you may well discover options such as the Greater Pittsburgh Special Hockey Association or the Washington Ice Dogs Hockey Team.

Special-needs "Challenger" baseball: A success story

Stan Jaskiewicz's son Peter is an 11-year-old with high-functioning autism. Stan is very involved in all his children's activities but has taken a particularly active role in ensuring positive community experiences for Peter. Here's Stan's take on his experience in coaching and helping to run special-needs sports programs:

> We started [Peter] in [typical] three-on-three soccer as a very young child. It was a fiasco because, even though it was small, I think soccer is such a fluid game. I don't think he could pick up on what was expected, so he'd just run around the field. It was a horrible experience. The other coaches wouldn't even talk to me.
>
> Instead, we've always done TOPSoccer (special-needs soccer), and that's been fantastic. And I run Challenger baseball league. Challenger baseball is a division of Little League; kids with any disabilities are included.
>
> My goal in running the program is not to teach the kids how to catch or hit a baseball; my goal is to let the kids have a good time outside, doing things together. It's different for every kid.
>
> Last year we had three young brothers—they were bouncing all over the place. I practiced just handing the ball down the line and back to me, and it took all season for them to do it! Another boy is brain-injured with some physical limitations; when he throws the ball, it can go in any direction. I'll just be silly with him to make him laugh—not everyone is there to play baseball; it's about having a good time.

Peter likes to hit the ball and run the bases. We don't keep score. Everyone is a winner in Challenger—no outs, no runs. We're not trying to move people into regular sports: we're trying to have a good time outside. If the families come back, we're successful.

Semi-inclusive and inclusive sports and the YMCA

Autism, of course, is a spectrum disorder, which means that your individual child with autism may be profoundly disabled or nearly typical. While special-needs sports are ideal for more profoundly disabled children and typical sports may be an option for children with Asperger syndrome, many children with autism are somewhere in between. Your child may be verbal and able to follow the rules of a game but unable to keep up with the fast pace of a team sport like soccer, hockey, football, or basketball.

If you (or your child with autism) are determined to get involved in team sports but it is not a good fit for special or typical team sport options, a good alternative is the YMCA.

There is no place like the YMCA. An international organization with locations around the world, today's YMCA is open to absolutely everyone, offering programs of every sort imaginable—most of them related to sports for toddlers, tweens, teens, and adults. What that means for families of children with autism is:

- Your child *and* your entire family are welcome, no matter how old, how disabled, how rich, or how poor. Every Y offers a financial-aid program, so money is no object.

- The vast majority of YMCAs are willing to include children with special needs in their programs, as long as inclusion is physically possible.

- Many YMCAs (possibly most) offer adapted swim programs for individuals with special needs.

- Your child with autism can't age out of the YMCA: babies and seniors alike are provided for.

- Your child with autism will find YMCAs no matter where he lives, and all Ys are similar. For a person with autism, this is a huge benefit.

- In addition to physical fitness and wellness, YMCAs around the world teach four "core principles" in the context of every program they offer, both to adults and to children. This means that coaches, teammates, and staff are all trained in *caring, honesty, respect,* and *responsibility.* This, for most parents, is no small thing.

Another great plus for the YMCA is that, unlike "special" sports programs, the Y's inclusive programs can prepare your child with autism for inclusion in typical sports activities. And YMCA programs are similar whether you're a toddler, tween, teen, or adult. What that means is that if your child has been "included" with support in toddler sports at the Y, he may then graduate to less fully supported sports as a tween and may even choose to get involved on his own as a teen and adult.

YMCAs also offer a variety of physical activities. So, unlike programs that focus on just one sport, you and/or your child can "migrate" to different sports to determine which is best for her. If basketball isn't a good fit, baseball or hockey might be. Or…through the YMCA or another recreation program, you and/or your child may determine that team sports just aren't for her. If you do, you might want to consider some of the many other individual and individual/team sports available either through the Y, through your recreation department, or through other sports-related venues.

Working with a coach and coaching your child

If you're hoping to have your child with autism included in a typical or semi-inclusive sports program, you'll almost certainly need to communicate with a volunteer coach. Volunteer coaches may or may not have much training at all, and even the best-trained coaches may have little or no background in or understanding of autism. It's not unusual for a volunteer coach (usually a dad) to know of autism only in the context of movies like *Rain Man* or from dramatic media stories. As a result, coaches may have a stereotypical vision of what to expect from your child. On the one hand, he may expect frightening or violent behaviors; on the other, he may expect outstanding and surprising talents.

Before taking the step of enrolling your child with autism in a sports program, therefore, it's a very good idea to start by communicating with your child's potential coach. After a conversation with the coach, you should have a good idea of whether your child and the volunteer coach are a good match.

Questions to ask a coach

- What is the goal of this team/league?
- Have you ever worked with an autistic child before?
- What is your feeling about including a child with autism on your team?
- If this league or team is part of a larger organization (Little League, for example), do you have any resources available to you from organizational headquarters?
- How would you feel about an aide or parent being present during practices and games to support my child with autism?
- Are you willing to make use of materials we provide to support our child with autism? (Often, parents can support their child with personalized visual charts, social stories, and other tools.)
- How would you handle _____? [Fill in the blank with behaviors or concerns that relate to your individual child.]

Questions for coaches to ask families

- What are your goals for your child relative to this sport?
- What are your concerns about his involvement in this team/league?
- Does your child have any sensory, communication, or behavior issues I should be aware of?
- If any of these issues arise, what's the best way to help your child cope?
- Can you or another support person be available during practices and games?
- Do you have any tools (toys, charts, etc.) that might help your child prepare for and take part in this team?

- What's the best way to communicate with you regarding questions or concerns?

Once you've determined that your child will get involved with a particular sports team, it's up to you, the parent, to prepare your child. Remember that typical kids are likely to have a head start on your child with autism. That's not just because your child is autistic. Bear in mind that when your child is in therapy sessions, doctors' offices, and social-skills groups, other kids are out there shooting hoops, kicking balls, and otherwise learning the physical and social skills of particular sports. As a good "autism parent," you may also be limiting the time your child spends in front of the television watching spectator sports and learning the rules of the game.

What that means is that your child will likely need a lot of preparation before even arriving at the playing field. Not only will he need to build his skills in kicking, throwing, running, and so forth, but he also will need basic information. What is a goal? What are you supposed to do with this ball? What are teammates, and how do you cooperate with them? What are the boundaries of the playing field? Even if your child with autism has been exposed to the sport you've chosen, it's quite possible that he didn't fully understand how and why the ball is moved up and down the field.

Start by asking the coach which skills she'll be focusing on and what your child will be expected to know or do. Ask what schedule she'll be following during each practice, so you can prepare your child. If you feel it's helpful, you might consider taking photos of the coach, the field, and the equipment—and creating a social story or cheat sheet so that your child can memorize the place and anticipate expectations.

Then get out there with your child and teach, practice, and have fun. Know that a child with autism may not have the attention span, competitiveness, or coordination of a typical child, which means your practice sessions may become brief, repetitive, and frequent. But that's okay, so long as both you and your child look forward to the experience. If, on the other hand, practicing with a parent, friend, therapist, or sibling becomes drudgery, it may make sense to set aside team participation for this season.

Best ideas for sports and the child with autism

Sports and physical activity are important for everyone. Kids, teens, and adults with autism are no exception. Sports can build health, muscle tone, and energy. Just as importantly, they can build confidence, self-esteem, and physical and social skills. Sports can be a great opportunity for family bonding. And where your child with autism may be below par in many settings, she may be exceptional in her sport of choice.

Rock climbing is a case in point. Many towns offer rock climbing through the schools, recreation centers, Ys, Jewish Community Centers (JCC), and other sports-oriented resources. Who would imagine their child with autism choosing such a sport? But consider the following:

- Rock climbing is an individual sport—no team engagement required.

- Rock climbing is intuitive. You climb the wall—no complex rules of engagement required.

- Rock climbers climb in a harness, and a belayer supports them with a rope. The sensation of the harness, for many youngsters, is akin to a weighted vest.

- Because the belayer is able to help the child climb (by pulling her up past a frustrating spot, for example), the child can be successful the first time.

- Succeeding in climbing a rock wall is a big deal for any kid. Many typical kids can't manage it. Yet I've watched more than one child with autism fearlessly scale several stories. Imagine the pride your child—and you—would feel after a successful climb!

Tom Cook rock climbing at Willy's World gym in Wallfleet, MA

Top sports tips

- Choose a sport that builds on your child's strengths and interests.

- Avoid sports that would create undue stress (highly competitive teams, sports that involve uncomfortable sensory experiences, etc.).

- Consider choosing nonteam sports or team sports that stress individual achievement (golf, swimming, etc.).

- Find or create a setting that meets your child's needs (special-needs programs, semi-inclusive programs, supported programs, etc.).

- Communicate directly with the leader or coach, letting him or her know your needs and determining whether he or she is likely to work well with your child.

- Prepare your child for the experience he's about to have, through social stories, photos, and practice.

- Be prepared to walk away if your child is stressed or if you are uncomfortable with the situation, and don't worry too much if you need to try several options before hitting the right match for your child.

- Allow your child to be challenged and to rise to the challenges presented.

- Be prepared to be surprised by your child's interests and abilities.

- Consider the possibility that your child's serious interest in a sport could lead to volunteer or even work opportunities.

Of course, your child with autism will face limits created by access, location, personal challenges, and personal preferences. But virtually every child with autism will find that some sport—swimming, running, hiking, throwing, dancing, karate—will work for him.

Tip sheet

On the next pages is a tip sheet that you should copy and share with coaches who will be working with your child or other children on the autism spectrum. You can also direct interested coaches to more great information available at the National Autistic Society site (U.K.): www.nas.org.uk/nas/jsp/polopoly.jsp?d=528&a=18382.

✓

Youth coach's tip sheet for welcoming kids and teens with autism

Congratulations! You have a new team member who is going to gain tremendously from his or her involvement in your organization. As the coach of the team, your leadership and support will make all the difference—not only to your new team member but also to his or her teammates and to the parents of all your team members.

As you develop your coaching plan, here are some tips to help you effectively include your team member with autism:

1. Know that every autistic kid is unique. If you've worked with an autistic child in the past, it's very possible that your new team member will surprise you.

2. Find out about your new team member. Ask his parents for any useful information they can provide about his special challenges and abilities. Be sure to ask about his past experiences with your sport—kids with autism may have fewer experiences with team sports than their typical peers.

3. If your new team member can tell you about herself, be sure to ask her whether she has any specific concerns or anxieties.

4. Start with the basics. You may believe that all the kids on your team are familiar with the equipment and basic goals of the game, but there's a good chance your autistic team member is not. If you're working with young children, there's even a chance that other team members could use a little refresher.

5. Use visual and hands-on teaching tools. You may be used to telling kids what they need to know—but kids with autism may have a tough time with verbal instructions. You can demonstrate, write down your instructions, or even offer hand-over-hand help so that your team member with autism really "gets" your message.

6. Give direct instructions. Some kids have great intuition about where the ball is going to be next or how to pass or accept a pass. Kids with autism don't. You'll need to be very direct in telling your team member with autism where to go, what to do, and when to do it. You may need to provide reminders to help her stay focused.

7. Be aware of possible sensory issues. Kids with autism may have unusual concerns about smells, loud noises, or physical sensations. That means your autistic team member's anxiety may be related to an itchy tag, a too-tight piece of equipment, sticky mud, or loud whistling. Of course, you can't get rid of all those issues; but by being aware of possible problems, you may be able to make things easier. It's quick and easy to cut a tag, loosen a buckle, or lower the intensity of your whistle.

8. Use other team members as peer buddies. Most teams include at least a few kids who are good at and enjoy helping others. If you can, team your autistic team member with a buddy who's willing to lend a helping hand. During breaks, the buddy or buddies can spend a little extra time coaching, practicing, or just hanging out with your autistic team member.

9. Use your autistic team member's parents as aides. It's quite possible that your autistic team member will need extra help in building sports skills. If you have the time and inclination, you can certainly work with him. But it's absolutely fine just to let his mom or dad know what skills to work on—and provide some hints and tips on how to help him build those skills. If necessary, you can even ask them to shadow their child during the practices and games.

10. Don't lower your expectations. It's tempting to allow a child with autism to do his own thing, even if his thing has nothing to do with your sport. But unless you run into serious behavior issues (which you should address with the child's parents), it's important to find a way to include your autistic team member in the game.

Chapter 5

Scouts, 4-H, the YMCA, and Other Youth Groups

Could your child with autism be a participating member of a youth group? Should she be? While youth groups aren't for everyone, your child may find a real home and group of friends through a secular or religious youth organization. If you do find the right fit, the results can be outstanding.

To find that right fit, it could take some hit-or-miss experimentation. The bad news is that group settings can be tough for kids with autism, even when the rules are clear and the setting is consistent. The good news is that many youth organizations and groups are becoming increasingly open to kids with differences. Just as importantly—and unrelated to the rise in special-needs diagnoses—most are becoming increasingly open to parent involvement and participation.

Why work to involve my child with a youth group?

As all parents of children on the autism spectrum know, it's critical for our kids to learn to socialize outside the autism classroom or therapeutic setting. A child who can respond beautifully to a therapist in a controlled, predictable situation may have no idea how to take that skill out into the wide world. This ability to generalize is really what therapies are all about: in the long run, autism therapy should prepare your child to take part in ordinary conversations, groups, and activities.

Some therapists do work toward the goal of generalization, but it isn't easy given all the limitations of time, space, and available settings in which to practice. Some therapists have extraordinarily busy schedules; others are limited by the strictures of the school setting. It sounds easy to practice social skills during recess, but if recess is only 15 minutes long or typical peers aren't available when your child is at recess, the opportunity can disappear quickly.

So what is the best way to help your child learn to use those social and behavioral skills outside a therapist's office? Your child knows the therapist or teacher will provide cues, extra time, and predictable responses. But what will a random child or adult do? No one really knows, least of all a child with autism. Typical kids learn flexibility through practice, and so will your child with autism.

Of course, kids with autism need extra preparation and support to do well in a new social situation. As a parent, it will be your job to help your child prepare, cope with social anxiety, and behave and engage to the best of his ability.

Structured youth groups and clubs—Scouts, 4-H, Adventure Guides, and so forth—are one good way to work on social- and group-interaction skills. They're predictable programs that offer structured activities, understandable procedures, and terrific opportunities for growth. They were also created with the goal of helping young people build confidence, social skills, and leadership abilities. If anyone can benefit from a program that's designed to build those skills, it's kids with autism.

Of course, it may not be easy or simple to include your child in any given group. As discussed previously, depending on your child's functional level and behaviors, you may or may not choose to reveal his diagnosis. Some parents prefer to use euphemistic terms such as *developmental delay, speech delay,* or *young for his age* instead of *autism,* since the "A-word" can bring up some scary images that may be irrelevant to your child's actual behavior or needs. Even if you don't use the word *autism* to describe your child, you'll certainly need to brief the leader on your child's needs and challenges. You may also decide, along with the leader, to brief other members of the group.

The good news, though, is that most major clubs and youth organizations are finally noticing that there are families out there with autistic kids who actively want to join up—and these organizations are working hard to support that interest.

Perhaps most importantly, getting your child with autism involved—really involved—with a youth program means he will have the chance to stretch his limitations—try on new ways of exploring the world, wear new clothes, perhaps even make connections that will last a lifetime.

My kid in Boy Scouts?! How traditional organizations are opening their doors

Organized youth programs are everywhere. In many families and communities, boys and girls join youth and community organizations such as Boy Scouts and Girl Scouts, 4-H, Girls and Boys Clubs, Girls Brigade, Sea Scouts, and so forth. Many other community organizations, such as the YMCA, Jewish Community Centers (JCC), and some philanthropic organizations offer special programs for youth. Most religious institutions (churches, synagogues) have youth groups intended for youngsters who have "graduated" from a structured religious-studies program but are too young to become full-fledged community members. These programs are intended to help boys and girls build character and values, friendships and collaboration skills, and physical skills ranging from sewing to orienteering.

Parents with kids on the autism spectrum may feel that it would be nice to have a place where their child can practice social and communication skills, but they wonder why in the world their child, who is still building basic communication skills, should get involved with camping or craft making or learning about civics. After all, isn't it more important to focus on basic life skills, rather than getting involved with something outside the realm of day-to-day activity? And besides, aren't most of those activities beyond the scope of kids on the autism spectrum?

The answer to these questions, of course, is "yes and no." Yes, of course, your child with autism needs to build basic skills. But there's so much more to life than the basics, and your child may well be readier to go for a hike, help out at a soup kitchen, or learn a song than he is to, say, perfect his handwriting or transition appropriately from homeroom to gym. Meanwhile, as your child struggles with basic conversation, he may be more than capable of working together with another individual or small group on a project that is of real, intrinsic interest.

Peter Jaskiewicz on a Boy Scounting trip

While all children can benefit from the experiences offered by these groups, children and teens with autism may actually be able to gain the most. After all, these organizations and programs are geared to teaching precisely the skills that our kids truly need: social communication, collaboration, and self-esteem. They also provide a structured environment in which to learn, connect, and discover.

Many parents assume that there's no place for their child with autism in these very traditional groups. They never saw any special-needs kids when they were Boy Scouts or Brownies. And so…they stay away in droves.

In fact, though, all these organizations are beginning to recognize the importance of serving youth with special needs. Some are starting to see families with autistic children as a growing market. And a few are actually devising specific programs and training to support the inclusion of children with special needs.

The reasons for this sea change are actually pretty straightforward.

First, there is a lowered interest among typical families in traditional community organizations. Rather than enroll their son in Boy Scouts, many parents of typical boys are choosing to focus on specialty programs and lessons. Instead of taking their children to the YMCA, parents are finding unique dance studios or tumbling gyms. Many of these older organizations have (or are believed to have) "old-fashioned" values, and some parents are uncomfortable with highly structured, conservative organizations. What all this means is that Boy Scouts, Girl Scouts, 4-H, the YMCA, and so forth are hungry for new members. They're more willing, therefore, to bend to the needs of families who are hungry for inclusion.

Second, community organizations are beginning to return to their roots—and their mission statements. Virtually all these organizations have missions that either directly or indirectly support the idea that all children—regardless of race, creed, or disability—deserve positive, enriching experiences led by caring adults. For

Ben, the happiest camper on earth

example, the website of the World Association of Girl Guides and Girl Scouts includes this note as part of a whole section dedicated to international work on inclusion:

> All girls and adults, regardless of ability, are welcome in Girl Scouting. The Girl Scouts organization is open to any girl with a disability until age 21 if she receives Special Education services until age 21.

And here's what Camp Fire USA has to say about its inclusive policies:

> As the first nonsectarian, interracial organization for girls in the United States, Camp Fire USA takes pride in its long-standing commitment to providing fun programs and services to all children and families in America. We are inclusive, open to every person in the communities we serve, welcoming children, youth and adults regardless of race, religion, socioeconomic status, disability, sexual orientation or other aspect of diversity.

Third, all these organizations are nonprofits. Nonprofits survive on donations and grants. Autism has become a focus of many philanthropic foundations, and a growing number of wealthy grandparents have grandchildren with autism. What that means is that, by opening their doors to children with autism, these institutions are better placed to raise more money. Funds made available for programs specific to children with autism can also help to fund positions, equipment, and space for institutions as a whole.

The bottom line for families living with autism, then, is that there are more and more opportunities for your child in community organizations than ever before. There's more awareness of developmental disabilities and more willingness to accommodate special needs. But you'll never know what's available in your local area unless you ask!

A case in point: Autism and the "new" Boy Scouts

Many dads of boys with autism grew up in Boy Scouting. Very few, if any, had disabled children in their Cub Scout packs or troops. As a result, few dads of boys with autism think of their sons as potential Boy Scouts. But times have changed.

Today, there are special-needs-only Boy Scout troops and Cub packs, and many children with special needs including autism are also included in typical Boy Scout groups. But that's just one aspect of the change that's come over Boy Scouting. Not only are the Boy Scouts—in the United States and elsewhere—more open to and supportive of boys with disabilities and special needs, but they are also far more open than ever before to involving parents of all boys in Boy Scouting activities.

A new program called "Scout Parents" invites moms and dads of typical and special-needs Scouts to take a paraleadership role with their child's troop or pack. This means that parents of a boy with autism can be on the spot during Scouting events—with a legitimate role to play outside of supporting their own son. What's more, even parents of typically developing boys now have the option of going along on trips, camping adventures, and even to summer camp; and many do. This is a huge plus, of course, for parents of children with autism who are nearly but not quite ready to manage typical Boy Scout activities on their own.

Frank Ramirez is a program specialist with Boy Scouts of America and part of the national Youth Development Team. In an interview, Frank told me:

> A Scout with autism is encouraged to take part in *all* pack activities—all activities of the district that the pack belongs to and all council events. Most councils have the yearly Scout-arama; all Scouts look forward to participating. There are councils that do offer Camporees for Scouts with special needs; certainly, a Scout with autism should be encouraged

to take part in those events as well. Almost every council that has a special-needs director is going to have a special-needs Camporee or some kind of event each year that welcomes all Scouts with disabilities. And most major metropolitan councils do have special-needs directors and the resources they need.

Joe Harrington, a Chicago-area Boy Scout leader with a long-standing interest in children with special needs, describes even more opportunities for children with autism and their families:

> Boy Scouts of America offers special needs training for scout leaders; every year they run a week-long course on working with Scouts with special needs. They have training material available and a book called *Working with Scouts with Special Needs*. Another program I'm trying to spread is "Champion Buddy"—you earn a patch by being a buddy with a scout or participating in activities we've developed. It's an intro to learning to help these kids out. I know a number of buddies who help out at summer camp.

Cubby Elder and three fellow Boy Scouts at the wilderness camp week at Chesterfield Scout Reservation, MA

> We also run a program for girls and boys called "Learning for Life" and another called "Venturing" for youth 14+, male or female, with or without special needs.
>
> These programs are of benefit to all the kids. It's a two-way street and a learning experience for everyone. Every year we have a picnic for about 1,000 disabled individuals of all ages. Boy Scouts come out and help—serve food, run games, and the same kids come out each year. They love to help out! We actually run out of space, with 200 Scouts volunteering to help out.

All this sounds fine and dandy from the point of view of the Boy Scout leadership. But what's it really like in the trenches for an autistic Boy Scout and his dad? In Chapter 2, we first met Stan Jaskiewicz's son, Peter, who is moderately autistic. Peter started out with the Cub

Scouts when he was in second grade. Here's Stan's take on the actual experience of parenting an autistic Boy Scout:

> When Peter was in second grade, he started with Cub Scouts at his school. I don't know what motivated him to go—Scouts were the last thing on my mind! Somehow, he was interested enough to go; the first year, I didn't participate much, but he seemed to enjoy it. So I got involved.
>
> We found that the clarity and consistency of Scouts, being able to stand up and get an award—all was highly motivating. You could see it on his face. The real test came in the summer of 2007 because, as you get higher in Scouts, there are some things you can only do in summer camp. I got CDs of nature sounds and started playing them at night; had him sleep on his bed in a sleeping bag—and he made it. He went to camp for two nights; other kids wanted to stay up and talk, and he went back to his mother's tent (she went with him). In our pack, at least half to three-quarters of the kids had parents go with them to summer camp.
>
> This past winter, Peter graduated from Cub Scouts. He had a wonderful experience.
>
> Next, of course, we had to find the right Boy Scout troop. To pick a Boy Scout troop, we visited the troop associated with our pack; it became clear that it wouldn't be a good fit for him. Just visiting, twice or three times someone came over to correct him. We went to an outdoor event; no one came over to talk to him.
>
> We visited other troops, including the troop at our church. We spoke with one of the leaders beforehand and explained about Peter's autism; and he said "I knew—I could tell," then introduced me to his son who has Down syndrome! He completely got it. It was a matter of being "them" versus being "us."
>
> It's a lot of work for me and for my wife. You can't just drop Peter off and go away. You have to participate, come along.
>
> The Boy Scouting experience for Peter has been astoundingly good: he's in there with other kids, they see him as doing well; he's just another Scout. A lot of that is because the leadership made that possible.

Why youth groups may be a good match for your child

If you've ever been part of a formal youth group, you know that most are quite ritualized, consistent, and predictable. Scouts start every meeting with a pledge. 4-H builds its programs around annual events that are always very much the same (county fairs, harvest festivals, and the like). Religious youth groups meet at church, run fundraisers, and attend denominational events that are generally very similar from year to year. With all that consistency, youth groups can be a very comfortable place for kids on the autism spectrum.

Most youth groups are also built around the idea that if you do X work, you receive Y award. For kids with autism, that kind of consistent, rule-oriented thinking can be very reassuring. Girl and Boy Scouts even earn merit badges and "recognitions" based on a clearly articulated set of expectations, placing achievement squarely in the hands of the Scout.

Youth groups typically focus on building leadership skills through public service and volunteerism. Kids with autism are often the beneficiaries of volunteerism but are rarely asked or expected to do for others. Certainly, therapists, teachers, and paraprofessional aides won't push your child with autism to consider helping others in need, cleaning up the local park, caring for stray animals, or otherwise taking an active role in improving the world around them. Yet children with autism are just as capable as anyone else of doing the right thing and making a difference in the world. As parents, don't we try to build leadership skills and community awareness in our typical children? Why not in our children with autism?

Youth groups are also all about team building. The whole point of joining organizations like Adventure Guides, Girl Scouts, or Camp Fire USA is to foster friendships, build an understanding of one's role in the larger world, and take responsibility for doing the right thing. They do this, in part, through nurturing relationships with parents, community leaders, and peers. Here, for example, is how the YMCA Adventure Guides describe themselves:

> We have designed the YMCA Adventure Guides program to assist you and your child on your journey of discovery. While activities with the whole family are important, we see tremendous value in supporting and strengthening the ability

of a parent and his or her child to communicate at an early age in ways that are caring, honest, respectful, and responsible.

Finding a youth group for your child with autism

Youth groups are run by churches and synagogues. They're the central focus of Boys and Girls Clubs, Scouts, YMCA Adventure Guide, Sea Scouts, 4-H, Campfire USA, Earth Scouts, and Civil Air Patrol. In the U.K., there's the Girls' Brigade, Woodcraft Folk, and London Youth. There are youth groups organized around interests, volunteer opportunities, and special skills. Which group is right for your child with autism?

You can easily eliminate some organizations right off the bat. If you're Jewish, you're not going to want to involve your child in a church group. If you have a daughter, Boy Scouts are out. You may feel that certain organizations are too far away, that the groups are too large, that the program is too demanding, and so forth. You may feel you want an organization that's very accepting of parent involvement (YMCA Adventure Guides is all about parent–child bonding) or you might want a group that will push your child toward building independence.

Once you've eliminated the obviously unacceptable choices, you'll have to dig a bit deeper. Some points to consider:

- What's easily available?
- Where do I (Mom or Dad) feel most comfortable?
- Which organization is likely to be of greatest interest to my child?
- Which organization runs its meetings or programs in a manner that's likely to be comfortable for my child?
- Which local organization has the most creative, supportive, inclusive leadership and/or membership?
- Which organization is most likely to support my child over time?
- Which organizations teach the skills, values, or ideals that I feel are important?

Of all these considerations, the quality of local leadership is probably the most significant. Your son may have no particular interest in (or even awareness of) 4-H, but if a terrific 4-H leader is running a program nearby, it's probably worth your while to check it out. The content of the program is of less significance than its quality—and for the child with autism, it's all about the ability of the leader to engage and include kids who don't always share their thoughts or wear their enthusiasm on their sleeve.

If you're not aware of local youth groups or have never gotten involved with any, it's easy to find a few through your local telephone directory or through Google. But before you even consider getting your child with autism involved, here are a few things to do:

- Read up on the organization. If you're not comfortable with the organization's beliefs, teachings, approach, or philosophy, it's probably not a great idea to get involved.

- Ask around about the local chapters of the organization. In particular, ask the parents of kids with autism. What you'll probably find is that certain local leaders are particularly good at inclusion, while others aren't. You'll quickly discover that leader A might be a terrific mentor for your child, while leader B is someone to avoid at all cost.

- Interview the local leader. Do you like him or her? How does he respond when you ask about his comfort level with disabled kids (or even kids with developmental delays)? Does he have specific ideas for how to engage a child who has a tough time connecting? How willing is he to listen to you or involve you in the organization?

- Visit a meeting without your child, and watch the dynamics among the children and between the children and the leader. Can you envision your child taking part in this group (even with support) and enjoying the experience? Can you imagine this group of kids reaching out to your child? Does the leader do a good job of reaching out to shy group members, or does she back off and allow more verbal kids to take over?

Once you've selected a group that looks right to you, it's time to prepare your child to meet the group. Depending on your child's needs, you may want to prepare a social story with photos (or a video) to provide a preview of the meeting experience. You may also choose to introduce your child slowly, by having him attend only the beginning of a meeting for a few weeks, and then take part in the activities with you as his shadow. In consultation with the group leader (and as possible with your child), you may want to provide other group members with ideas on how best to relate to and include your child. Slowly, you may be able to pull back—until, over time, you're able to "disappear" into the shadows…and, finally, just drop your child off and wave good-bye.

Should I lead my own youth group?

It's perfectly possible that, no matter how hard you search, you'll find no appropriate youth group in your area. Or—even more likely— you'll find no leader who really has a clue how to include a child with autism. If that's the case, one viable option is simply to start up your own group. You can become a Cub Scout leader, start a youth group at your church, or become the first local Camp Fire leader in your area. There are major pros and cons to this approach, and only you know whether you can handle the double challenge of managing a youth group while also supporting your autistic child.

The up-side to starting your own youth group is control. You started it; therefore, you can decide when it will run, where it will meet, how structured it will be, what kinds of activities you'll undertake, and so forth. That means you can actually design your youth group to meet the special needs of your autistic child. And since you're in charge, there's no issue about inclusion, no question about whether your child has what it takes to be a part of the group, and no concerns about possible conflicts with the group leader.

The down-side to starting your own youth group (outside of the time, energy, and commitment involved) is the reality that you'll need to split your time and attention among *all* the group members. That means that if your child with autism is having a hard time with a project, a person, or a situation, you may not have the freedom to focus on her special needs. After all, there are other kids' needs to consider too.

Of course, there are ways to get around some of the difficulties inherent in running your own youth group. For example, you can share the load with another parent, team your autistic child with a sibling or peer buddy, focus your activities around your child's personal strengths, or hire a teen to support your child throughout each meeting. But no matter how you slice it, if you are a youth group leader, you owe it to the group to serve all the kids—not just the one in your own family.

Top tips for youth groups, clubs, and kids with autism

- Know that not every program, group, or leader will be right for your child. You may have to shop around or go far afield to find that perfect match.

- Consider your child's interests and personality. She may be the kind of kid who can thrive in rule-based, uniform-wearing groups—or not. She may be interested in groups with a special focus, be it religious, agricultural, or artistic.

- Decide whether you want to reveal your child's diagnosis. Whether you do or don't, have a plan for managing any concerns, problems, or issues that arise as a result of your child's autism.

- You may have to grow a thick skin. Your child is autistic, and that means that other kids in the group may stare or tease, that the group leader may be confused or concerned about your child's behavior, or that your child may not achieve as much as the other kids in the group. If your child is having a positive experience, though, you may need to take a deep breath and simply cope.

- Consider taking a slow, gentle approach to getting started. A visual introduction (photos or video) is a great way to start. It's okay to shadow your child for a while or to attend only a portion of meetings until your child is comfortable.

- Think long and hard about whether you want to start your own youth group. If you do go that route, be sure your child will have the support he needs from someone other than you.

Tip sheet
On the next pages is a tip sheet that you should copy and share with organization leaders who will be working with your child or other children on the autism spectrum.

✔

Youth group leader's tip sheet for welcoming kids and teens with autism

Congratulations! You have a new youth-group member who is going to gain tremendously from his or her involvement in your organization. As the group leader, your example and support will make all the difference—not only to your new group member but also to other group members and their parents.

As you develop your plan for the group as a whole, here are some tips to help you effectively to include your group member with autism:

1. Know that every autistic kid is unique. If you've worked with an autistic child in the past, it's very possible that your new group member will surprise you.

2. Find out about your new group member. Ask his parents for any useful information they can provide about his special challenges and abilities. Be sure to ask about his past experiences with group-oriented activities—kids with autism may have fewer experiences than their typical peers.

3. If your new group member can tell you about herself, be sure to ask her whether she has any specific concerns or anxieties.

4. Start with the basics. Your new group member may know very little about your organization, your rules for group participation, your schedule, or your goals. Of course, it's always nice to have seasoned members of your group explain the details.

5. When you introduce a new project, idea, or plan, be sure your autistic group member is really paying attention and understanding what you have to say. If possible, use visual and hands-on teaching tools. You may be used to telling kids what they need to know, but kids with autism may have a tough time with verbal instructions. You can demonstrate, write down your instructions, or even offer hand-over-hand help with hands-on projects so that your group member with autism really "gets" your message.

6. Give direct instructions. Kids with autism don't always understand expressions like "use your words" or "work nicely together." You'll need to be very direct in telling your team

member with autism where to go, what to do, and when to do it. For example, you may need to tell your new group member "When you've finished the first part of the project, it's okay to go on to the next step." You may need to provide reminders to help her stay focused.

7. Be aware of possible sensory issues. Kids with autism may have unusual concerns about smells, loud noise, or physical sensations. That means your autistic group member's anxiety may be related to an uncomfortable uniform, sticky glue, or a buzzing fluorescent light. Of course, you can't get rid of all those issues—but by being aware of possible problems, you may be able to make things easier. It's quick and easy to loosen a too-tight belt, offer a glue stick instead of a bottle of liquid glue, or switch on an incandescent light.

8. Use other group members as peer buddies. Most groups include at least a few kids who are good at and enjoy helping others. If you can, team your autistic group member up with a buddy who's willing to lend a helping hand. During breaks, the buddy or buddies can spend a little extra time coaching, practicing, or just hanging out with your autistic group member.

9. Use your autistic group member's parents as aides. It's quite possible that your autistic team member will need extra help in completing projects or preparing for events. If you have the time and inclination, you can certainly work with him. But it's absolutely fine to just let his mom or dad know what skills to work on—and provide some hints and tips on how to help him build those skills. If necessary, you can even ask them to shadow their child during meetings or events.

10. Don't lower your expectations. It's tempting to allow a child with autism to do his own thing—even if his thing has nothing to do with your organization's goals. But unless you run into serious behavior issues (which you should address with the child's parents), it's important to find a way to include your autistic group member in all your activities and events. In fact, your autistic group member may even surprise you with hidden talents, abilities, or strengths

Chapter 6

Museums, Zoos, Aquariums, and More

It's tough enough getting kids with autism in and out of the grocery store, the doctor's office, and the bathroom. You're fighting battles with schools, insurance companies, and social-service agencies. Why in the world would you want to get your child with autism into a museum, zoo, or aquarium?

You might be surprised to discover that museums are increasingly destinations for families with kids on the autism spectrum—and not just families with high-functioning kids, either. In part, that's because families are reaching out to partner with museums for special programs, resources, and training. In part, it's because museums are reaching out and doing the groundwork on their own. And in part, it's because families are realizing that museums are often wonderful places for parents, siblings, and the child or teen with autism.

What could possibly attract museums and families with autism to one another? It may help to explain that "museums" are much, much more than repositories of fine art (though, of course, they're that, too). In today's world, museums are about both education and entertainment, and they come in many "flavors." Most museums offer much more than static exhibits; the possibilities include hands-on pretend play, live animal shows, science workshops, engineering challenges, volunteer opportunities, overnight "camp-ins," auditorium shows, IMAX movies, planetarium presentations, arts-and-crafts classes, social clubs, special-interest clubs, concerts, tours, physical challenges—in other words, the possibilities are nearly endless.

There are children's museums loaded with hands-on activities, climbing structures, indoor playgrounds, and opportunities for building symbolic play and social skills. While these can be overwhelming for some kids with autism, they can also be wonderful resources. Some children's museums are now offering after-hours events for special-needs families; some have quiet times when very few people are in the galleries. There are even a few children's museums that have embraced families with autism to the point where they have trained their staff to support the needs of kids on the spectrum.

There are science museums where children, teens, and adults can climb through giant "hearts," build remote-control robots with Lego and K'Nex, climb inside jet engines, and explore the mysteries of internal combustion engines. Often, kids and teens with autism (particularly those with Asperger syndrome) are attracted to science museums as a paper clip is attracted to a magnet. And why not?

Tom Cook in the bay of a military plane during a public school field trip to Otis Air Force Base in Bourne, MA

Science-museum programs—and educators—are all about passion for science, technology, engineering, and hands-on discovery. Recently, science museums have begun to realize that they've always embraced people with autism—and many are making a deliberate effort to reach out to parents, provide supports, and generally make themselves available to the autism community.

There are cultural museums offering kids a chance to "step back in time" into recreations of colonial towns, warships, and cities of the past. Kids don't have to behave "appropriately" (that is, stay quiet or wait in line) at the Plimoth Plantation or Mystic Seaport. Instead, they're invited to wander into houses, plop down on other people's beds, explore, watch, and try. Even if your child doesn't come home spouting reams of historic knowledge, she will have had an opportunity to take part in a community-based experience that's likely to be positive and engaging. Meanwhile, you and your other children will have a chance to explore a cultural site that you've always wondered about.

Zoos, aquariums, and arboretums are also part of the larger "museum" world. Of course, everyone knows about zoos and aquariums, but did you know that most aquariums invite kids actually to pick up and touch tide-pool critters or to stroke a shark? Have you explored children's zoos where kids can actually feed and pet the animals, ride on elephants and camels, or climb inside a "cave?" And these days, even public gardens are becoming hands-on, bodies-on, interactive centers of learning. Some public gardens boast kid-friendly tree houses, model railways (yes, model railways!), water features, and other elements that kids and teens with autism find intriguing.

And remember that old-fashioned art museum? While some are still "adult-only" bastions, many are finding ways to engage kids through audio-video interpretations, large-scale interactive works of art, hands-on arts-and-crafts workshops, and more. Art museums can be a tough nut to crack for any child: no matter how open-minded they are, no art museum will allow kids to touch the Monets or climb on the Calders. But if New York's Metropolitan Museum of Art can make their galleries accessible to people with autism, it seems reasonable that other museums can and will follow suit.

If you have a child with autism, it's very likely that one or more of the types of museums I've described sounds like something your child would enjoy, assuming that you could prepare him for the experience and help him to manage the sometimes overwhelming sensory overload. This chapter includes a number of ideas for preparing your child for the museum and the museum for your child and also describes existing opportunities for special-needs families to visit the museum during the evening and other quiet times.

But fun and enjoyment are just part of the reason to involve your child in the world of museums. Another reason to become involved is for yourself and your other children: all of you deserve the opportunity to take advantage of the cultural and scientific opportunities in your community, and you may well find that museums are open to you in a way you'd never anticipated. The most important reason to get involved with museums, though, is this: your child may discover that he can learn, interact, explore, and even connect with others in museums, even if he can't achieve those goals in school.

Museums, multisensory learning, and the child with autism

Some kids with autism are natural museumgoers. Our son Tom fell in love with Philadelphia's Academy of Natural Sciences when he discovered the dioramas. Dioramas are glass-fronted cases containing re-creations of natural scenes, including taxidermy animals, painted backdrops, and reconstructions of trees, bushes, and other elements of the scene. Created originally to help visitors envision the wilderness before the invention of television or movies, dioramas now seem like boring throwbacks—to everyone except museum professionals, history buffs, and kids with autism.

What's so great about the dioramas? For one thing, they contain animals. Tom loves animals. In fact, one could say that biology is one of his passions.

For another thing, dioramas are visual teaching tools. They're three-dimensional visual representations of a real-world environment. But unlike the high-energy video games and TV shows that appeal to most typically developing kids, dioramas are also quiet, static exhibits. For Tom, this means he can use his talent for visual learning without having to follow fast-moving verbal direction. And because typical kids don't enjoy dioramas very much, he's usually able to spend many minutes visually exploring without being pushed or shoved by other kids who want their turn.

And dioramas are predictable. Every time we visit the museum, there the dioramas are, just as they've always been—since about 1920. For Tom, dioramas have been a terrific educational tool. Because of them, he has learned what types of animals live in different habitats, what those animals eat and how they live, and whether the animals are predators or prey. He can envision the Desert of Borkou in his imagination, and rattle off the names of several different species of antelope and turtle, their food, and their habits.

Some kids with autism, of course, are not natural museumgoers. Their sensory needs, attention span, anxiety, or other issues get in the way. But by and large, museums (broadly defined) have an awful lot to offer kids with autism.

Why are museums often a good match for kids on the autism spectrum? The answer lies in the educational approach used by museums, zoos, aquaria, and other informal teaching institutions.

Tom Cook with sister Sara at the train museum in Boothbay Harbor, ME

Unlike schools, museums have always operated on the assumption that visitors learn through *all* their senses. As a result, they have always designed their exhibits, programs, workshops, and classes to be interactive, multisensory, and open-ended. So, unlike school, museums are already set up to support your child's learning style—whatever that may be. Visual, aural, kinesthetic, musical, mathematical, observational, or other approaches to communication aren't provided for your child because he's "special": they're provided to everyone because that's just how museum education is done.

Schools—after preschool and kindergarten—prefer that kids learn verbally. Information is presented orally and is written in books. Learners must be able to listen to and process verbal information quickly, tap into knowledge already available in their heads, and prepare a verbal or written response. Since verbalization is intrinsically difficult for all children with autism—and impossible for some—school-based learning can become a nightmare.

All this is true despite the fact that we know that there are many different ways of learning and despite the fact that educators are taught about different learning styles. Back in the 1980s, as I've mentioned previously, Howard Gardner wrote a book called *Frames of Mind*, which outlined seven different learning styles—verbal, visual, aural, kinesthetic, musical, mathematical, and social—and just recently he added another to the list, "natural." If you know a child with autism, you know that his learning style is far more likely to be nonverbal than otherwise. What that means, of course, is that kids with autism are at a distinct disadvantage in the schools, and that disadvantage increases as your child gets older and education becomes less multisensory and more and more verbal.

In a museum—any museum—the assumption is that the visitor will explore only what interests him. And in most museums, the expectation is that the learner will use multiple senses to experience exhibits. Verbal communication skills are rarely the key to enjoying museum exhibits, zoos, aquaria, or gardens. In fact, it's perfectly possible for anyone, autistic or not, to spend hours exploring and enjoying a museum without ever reading a syllable or exchanging two words with another person. Sometimes visitors communicate nonverbally; in some museums, visitors may even be encouraged to work together on activities or experiments. But even in those circumstances, the ability to communicate verbally is not the key to success.

Tips for preparing your child (and yourself) for a museum visit

Some museums already make special accommodations for kids and families living with autism, and you'll read about a few specific autism-friendly museum programs later in this chapter. Assuming, though unlikely, that your local children's museum or zoo has heard the word *autism* only in the context of the movie *Rain Man*, how do you prepare your child for a museum visit?

First, choose your first museum visit with care. If your child has shown no interest in art, why start with an art museum? Preview (in person or on the Web) the museums, zoos, aquariums, etc., in your area. Ask friends with autistic kids which museums seem most interesting and tolerant. And while you're considering your autistic child's interests and needs, consider your own. If you, your spouse, or other children hate science museums but love zoos, there's really no good reason to make the science museum your first destination.

Second, choose your visit time wisely. Good times to visit the museum are *not* weekdays from 10a.m. to 1p.m., since that's prime school-group time. Saturday and Sunday afternoons are often crowded. Your best bet for a quiet, low-key museum experience is to show up as the doors open on Sunday morning. Second best is after 1p.m. on a weekday afternoon.

Museums also have "seasons." Never visit the Smithsonian in summer—and stay away from zoos on lovely summer and fall afternoons. Never, under any circumstances, visit a children's museum during winter vacations! Instead, try visiting big aquariums in the dead of winter, zoos in March or November, and indoor museums on perfect beach days.

Third, prepare your child for the visit. Every museum has a website, and every museum's website includes pictures, lists of exhibits, information about programs and events, and more. You may even find a map of the building online. Depending upon your child's abilities, you may want to plan your visit together; at the very least, you can print out images of the building and the exhibits you plan to visit and spend some time preparing for the experience.

Fourth, prepare for the possibility that your child may not have a good first experience—or may melt down relatively quickly even if he's having fun. In other words, be mentally and physically prepared to leave at a moment's notice—with no regrets. There's a very simple way to do this: rather than paying for an expensive one-time ticket, pay less by either (1) getting a discount ticket through your local library, or (2) buying a membership (often a surprisingly good deal that includes not only free admission but also free parking and discounts on food and purchases). We found that our son could only take so much of even his favorite museums—but because we had a membership, we didn't mind leaving after 45 minutes since we knew we could return for free anytime. Members also get invitations to member-only events, which may be less crowded than general-admission times.

Fifth, scout out critical facilities and locations ahead of time. Know where the bathroom is, know when and where you're going to eat, and know where you'll head to find quiet and privacy if your child does melt down. You can also call the museum ahead of time to ask about any special services for people with disabilities.

Sixth, relax. If your child with autism has a wonderful time petting the goats at the zoo and then melts down when a peacock squawks or spreads its tail, you've made a good start. If she decides to spend half

Fun and sun at the San Diego Zoo

an hour watching fish in the big tank at the aquarium but resists exploring the rest of the exhibits, watch with her—there's no need to cover the entire building in one visit. Remember that, while museums are rich resources for kids on the spectrum, they're still new and different settings with strange smells, sounds, and transitions. And what fascinates your child may or may not fascinate you. That's the beauty of exploring new places together.

Seventh and last, know that some museums just aren't autism (or even kid) friendly. Even when you've checked things out carefully, you may get dirty looks or requests to shush or remove your child. If that happens, I recommend that you either leave or remediate the situation on the spot. Then, if you like, write a letter to the president of the institution. Some parents have been very successful in bringing attention to their children's needs—and have even worked with museums to bring in autism specialists to train museum staff.

How museums prepare themselves for kids with autism

Not every museum has a special interest in attracting families with autistic kids. But as the number of families with kids on the spectrum grows, museums are beginning to see the writing on the wall. Meanwhile, quite a few museum board members now have grandchildren on the spectrum, and more and more foundations are willing to give philanthropic grants in support of programs for children and families with special needs. Given all these sea changes, it's not surprising that a growing number of museums of all sorts are working to become more accessible to kids with autism. The "case studies" below are just the tip of the iceberg; you'll find suggestions on how to work with your local museum later in this chapter.

Case study: Autism and the museums of Naperville, Illinois

Autistic children tend to be highly visual learners. Some, in fact, have photographic memories. Visual schedules are used in school settings to help autistic kids anticipate transitions, and visual teaching tools are staples for their teachers. And so, when the Illinois Autism Training and Technical Assistance Project approached Sandy Trusewych of the Dupage Children's Museum with the idea of a visual system for introducing autistic children to the museum's exhibits, Sandy was intrigued.

The idea was simple and straightforward: a set of visual guidebooks to prepare children and families to experience the museum, its exhibits, and its hands-on experiences. Wendy Partridge of the Autism Training and Technical Assistance Project explains:

> Our project funded the creation of the books. I went to the museum, along with a typical child who was homeschooled, and took pictures of the child going through the exhibits. Then we sat down with the museum staff and broke down the tasks. We created visual systems for various play schemes at exhibits like stream tables and construction zones. Once they get a gist of how to work at the stream table, they'll come up with their own creative play.

In addition to the photo books, which are available on loan for several exhibits, Sandy instituted a series of parent-training programs:

> We developed a monthly event called Third Thursday. From 5–7p.m., we invite families with autistic kids to visit the museum and keep the museum open to all families. We put together some additional supports to make the families more comfortable and at ease; our staff took an in-service on autism to learn about hallmark behaviors, so that the staff felt more prepared. Also, every month we invite professionals from the communities to cohost the evenings. We set up a resource table for parents to say hello and get information about books, workshops, seminars, and articles. My cohost brings agencies' information, too. It's been hugely popular; not that we get scores of families, but about five to ten families come in for a couple of Third Thursdays. All it took was an invitation. Sometimes they join, sometimes they don't—but this becomes a comfortable place for them.

Sandy notes that there have been very few negative incidents at the museum. Families come from as far as 50 miles away to visit, and a few have actually responded with tears of joy at a positive reception for their entire family—including their autistic child.

The Dupage Children's Museum is only one of several Illinois museums that have accepted the challenge of the Visual Systems program. The Brookfield Zoo and Discovery Center have also signed on, creating photo books for several of their exhibits. The Discovery Center, part of the TEAMS exhibit collaborative, has also made Visual Systems photo books an integral part of their traveling sports exhibit, "Team Up!"

Case study: Accessible art at the Metropolitan Museum

As early as 1987, New York's Metropolitan Museum of Art was concerned about making fine art accessible to learners with developmental delays. Based on the museum's existing family programs, Discoveries combines small groups and multisensory teaching techniques to reach and teach children and adults with a wide range of "differences." Presented in galleries and classrooms, Discoveries programs address many of the same themes as are addressed in typical educational programs at the Met—but they address them a bit differently.

Deborah Jaffe, the museum's access coordinator, describes the many ways in which the Discoveries team works to engage all their visitors:

> We do a lot of sketching, which allows nonverbal folks to respond to what they're seeing. We try to break down the "I can't draw" barrier. There's a lot of question/answer as opposed to lecture. We do some acting out of sculpture. We use material bags—pass around a piece of marble, bring in the other senses. When we did a program on art and emotion, we incorporated music; we used a classroom space to play different types of music to evoke different emotions. We had families drawing at the same time, telling them, "Use your crayon to draw the feeling you hear!" We grab everyone in every way possible.

Jaffe describes the Discoveries audience as varied. "We get lots of LD (learning disabled) kids and kids with ADHD/ADD, autism, and Down syndrome. Our adults are generally coping with traumatic brain injury and other disabilities."

But disabled individuals make up a surprisingly small part of the Discoveries audience.

Attendees arrive with families, groups, friends, and spouses. Many programs include as many as 25 people—with only four or five having learning differences. This means that other family members, including parents and siblings, have the opportunity to benefit from the multisensory approach.

Jaffe notes that many family members get a lot from their Discoveries experience: "When we first started using material bags [bags containing marble and other sculptural materials], parents said, "It really helps *me*!" Just as significantly, families appreciate the opportunity to attend a program together—rather than sending a disabled family member off to a specialized event or program.

Not only do the multisensory Discoveries teaching techniques help attending families make the most of the museum experience, but they also support the work of the museum's education staff as a whole. Says Jaffe, "My colleagues and I talk at general education meetings about using touch and other multisensory techniques as teaching tools. The Discoveries approach has filtered into different programs throughout the education program."

The Discoveries team has begun to work with other New York museums to develop similar multisensory programs. "It's not that difficult to do," says Jaffe. "For good educators—it's not magic. You have to call on a few tools you might not initially think of, but you don't need a special-education background or extensive training. You can reach people in different ways; you just need to adjust expectations. I'd like to encourage people to reach out to everyone!"

How to help your museum reach out to the autism community

If you're interested in working with your local museum to help its staff reach out to the autism community, you may or may not find a receptive ear. In recent years, more and more museums have started to think much more seriously about accessibility, though, so the likelihood of success is increasing every day. At the end of this chapter, you'll find a tip sheet for museum professionals that you can copy and share. Meanwhile, here are a few ideas to get you started.

BE SURE YOU'RE TALKING TO THE RIGHT PERSON

The director of education or visitor services is far more likely to be helpful than a gallery docent (who is probably a volunteer). Even better, try to get a meeting with both the hands-on gallery director and the director of the museum itself. Of course, this advice is not useful if you're dealing with a very large institution like the Smithsonian; in that case, you can actually work with the person who manages disability access.

MAKE IT CLEAR THAT YOU'RE NOT ASKING FOR THE WORLD

Kids with autism don't need expensive new equipment or facilities. What they do need—for the most part—are (1) a time during the week or month when they and their families can visit and expect relative quiet and calm, (2) a designated quiet room to which they can "escape" when necessary, and (3) a photo book and/or video that previews the museum experience. Point your local museum to the institutions that have already done this, so the staff can see they don't have to reinvent the wheel.

LET THE MUSEUM KNOW THAT YOU WOULD BE THRILLED TO HELP THEM MARKET THEIR INSTITUTION TO THE AUTISM COMMUNITY

Also let them know that it might even be possible to find professionals or parents willing and able to provide extra resources or support during special evening events.

LET THE MUSEUM KNOW THAT IT MIGHT BE POSSIBLE TO GET A GRANT TO SUPPORT AN AUTISM-FRIENDLY PROGRAM

Explain that many of the services you're requesting for your families will be equally useful for many school groups and for families whose kids have related developmental differences (ADHD, Tourettes, etc.).

In short, make it clear to your local museum that inviting families like yours to become paying customers isn't just the right thing to do—it's good for business, and it's good for fundraising. Provide them with the tools they need to help you. And know that it's possible that, despite your best efforts, they may say no. If that happens, a letter-writing campaign is always an effective option!

Museum programs, volunteer opportunities, and kids with autism

Museums do more than present exhibits. They also create programs, summer camps, volunteer opportunities, and family workshops. Some museums make a serious effort to include kids with autism in their programs and events; others are simply autism-friendly entities. Museum programs are not usually good options for kids who are nonverbal or unable to sit still, focus, or follow instruction. For those autistic kids and teens that are interested and able to take part, however, the opportunities are truly exciting. Some autistic teens have become valued volunteers and even employees at museums where their very focused passions and abilities are highly valued.

If you do decide to take part in a museum workshop, camp, class, or program—and you want to have your autistic child included fully—it's important to let the program director know of your child's special needs. In fact, the more information you can share, the better the museum will be able to prepare for your child. Of course, you'll also want to prepare your child for the experience—which may mean an advance visit to the program space, along with a chance for your child to ask any questions she may have about the experience.

One museum that welcomes kids with autism to their programs is the Science Museum of Minnesota. Science museums overall are now recognizing that kids and teens with Asperger syndrome and high-functioning autism have always been a part of their audience. In fact, it may be fair to say that kids on the spectrum make up some of the most passionate members of science museums—and can become some of the most effective volunteers and docents available. Up until now, though, museums never really gave much thought to the support such kids might need as they deal with peers, new situations, or stress. Now, thanks to greater autism awareness, they're making the effort—with positive results.

Kit Wilhite is director of Youth and Family Programs at the Science Museum of Minnesota. Her museum has included kids with autism in typical programs and camps for years, determining that autism-only programs are not in the best interest of either the museum or the participants. To prepare her staff, Kit contracts with the local Autism Society to provide training; training includes recommendations of strategies such as the use of visual schedules, warnings prior to transitions, and general background on autism and its challenges. Here are some of Kit's insights on including kids with autism and science museum programs:

> There are a lot of great scientists and engineers on the autism spectrum, and this area is really high interest for the kids. I was raised to be an inclusive educator; everyone on our team is on the same page on this. These kids deserve to be here. Every kid's an individual.
>
> When we see on a class roster that there's a child with an ASD, we call the parents and ask which strategies work best. We know to ask about sensory issues. Our staff is so bought in now that everyone calls. Recently, we heard from a local autism group that parents were recommending our summer-camp program. We're super-proud of that. We have a good reputation with parents of kids with life-threatening allergies, too. One parent recently told me that we're more progressive in that area than a lot of out-of-school organizations.
>
> There are significant benefits to us: this is part of our audience; we need to meet their needs. We're growing an audience by working positively with parents. We don't have a huge marketing budget, so word of mouth is very important. For our program to survive, we do what we can to be welcoming to families. It's an area of education that's interesting and important. We get tons of kids in our technology program— they're a brain trust! We want to grow more scientists, educators and engineers—it's part of our mission. We want everyone to be scientifically literate. We're passionate about that!

In addition to programs offered for youth, some museums offer leadership and volunteer opportunities. Young people with autism are often welcome to take part—and quite a few have had truly remarkable experiences with hands-on training in everything from live animal handling to fossil collection and cleaning to event management to collections management. As with museum programs, museum volunteering is not for teens whose autism-spectrum disorder makes them unable to communicate verbally or follow direction; but for the right teen, the opportunities are quite exciting. In fact, museum volunteering can easily lead to paid part-time and even full-time employment—and experiences offered through volunteering can prepare young people for higher education and/or jobs in a field of real interest.

The Academy of Natural Sciences in Philadelphia is one of those museums that combines exhibits and programs with behind-the-scenes scientific research. Its vast collections include bugs, birds, fossils, and bones—a wealth of fascination for some teens on the spectrum. The academy has always opened its volunteer program to teens, and over the years (as they now realize), many teens on the autism spectrum have come through their doors. Recognizing this trend, Director of Education Jacquie Genovese has made it a point to provide her staff with autism training to support aspiring volunteers on the spectrum.

Tom Cook on a homeschool field trip to catch and tag monach butterflies in Westport, RI

According to Jacquie, who has presented programs on the subject of autistic museum volunteers at the American Association of Museums, kids on the autism spectrum have successfully gone through volunteer training and become great assets to the museum. Surprisingly, she says, kids with autism aren't always best or most comfortable behind the scenes. While some have taken quickly to working with scientists on collections and databases, others have become dinosaur docents, live animal handlers, and "Camp In" (overnight at the museum) staff.

The key to success, says Jacquie, is communication with museum staff. Parents should double-check that their local museum even works with teen volunteers (some museums simply insist that volunteers must be over 18). Once you know the possibility is there for volunteering, parents need to let staff know, up front, what their child's abilities and needs are. Another key (sometimes tricky for kids on the spectrum) is flexibility. "Parents and kids need to be open to the possibility that their first choice of volunteer placement won't work out," says Jacquie. "If they're willing to try different settings, they may discover new interests and abilities."

Top tips for museum, zoo, or aquarium inclusion

- Choose the museum and the time of your visit with care. Make the choice based both on practical concerns (what's open, what's near, etc.) but also on your family's real interests.

- Prepare your child for the visit with photos or video, and be clear on where you're going and what you're going to do when you arrive.

- Know that your first visits may be brief, and plan accordingly by using discounted tickets or library passes. Have a plan in place for managing meltdowns or other behavior issues.

- Be flexible enough that if your child is really attracted by or interested in an exhibit, you can stop and enjoy it. No need to rush through!

- If you're interested enough to work toward creating a support program at your local museum, connect with the education department of the museum and join forces. Consider sharing resource people and materials (such as the tip sheet at the end of this chapter), so that the museum personnel can get a better feeling for how easy and inexpensive it really is to make accommodations for families with autistic members.

Tip sheet

On the next pages is a tip sheet that you should copy and share with museums, zoos, aquariums, and other professionals who will be working with your child or other children on the autism spectrum.

Museum professional's tip sheet for welcoming kids and teens with autism

Congratulations! You will soon be welcoming a new visitor or group who will gain tremendously from your museum's exhibits and programs. As a museum professional, you know that people learn in many ways; this tip sheet will help you tailor your program or presentation to the special needs of people on the autism spectrum.

1. Know that kids and teens with autism have been regular visitors to your museum for years. They look just like everyone else and often show a passion for your exhibits and collections that goes far beyond that of typically developing children.

2. If you've had only limited experience with autism, be aware that autistic symptoms vary widely from person to person. Not every autistic person has disruptive behaviors—in fact, many people with autism will want to become members and visit your museum over and over again.

3. Accommodating kids with autism and their families is neither difficult nor expensive. A basic set of accommodations include (a) a designated "quiet room," marked on your map, where families can go if a child becomes overwhelmed; (b) a set of photos or a video that parents can use to prepare their child for a museum visit; (c) information about which hours, exhibits, programs, and events are most likely to be quiet, low key, and tolerant of kids with developmental differences.

4. It's also important to make your staff aware that kids and families with autism may need a little extra help or support as they navigate the museum.

5. If you're interested in doing more for special-needs families, you can provide autism training for your staff (check with parent groups or with the local Autism Society of America chapter for information about trainers and funding). Some museums also offer occasional "special-needs nights" when families with autistic kids can visit and expect the museum to be quieter than usual.

6. There are a large and growing number of families with autistic children in your community. It's in your interest to accommodate their needs within reason since many will become members—and recommend membership to friends and family.

7. Funding in the form of grants is available to museums interested in accommodating the needs of kids with autism. These grants can, for example, help to support purchase of equipment, design of exhibit elements, program planning, and more.

For more information, you can contact the Autism Society of America—or, even better, connect with local parent support groups. You'll find some wonderful people and opportunities for doing well by doing good—right in your community.

Chapter 7

Autism and Faith Communities

You'd think inclusion in places of worship would be a no-brainer. After all, who would want to exclude a child from a place of worship?

Of course, as many of us already know, it's not that simple. The barriers to inclusion are very real, and they include everything from tradition and theology to lack of resources to sheer cluelessness. Today, though, the number of families with kids on the autism spectrum (and with other, similar special needs) is so significant that places of worship are taking real notice. Families, too, are becoming far more vocal about their needs and desires. Rather than simply staying away or providing their child with special needs with a religious education at home, families are insisting that places of worship find a way to include their child.

In some cases, the insistence goes a bit over the top. For example, when one family brought their very loud, out-of-control autistic teen to church services week after week, the congregation was understandably concerned. The pastor offered to work with the family to find a way to include their son without disrupting worship for the rest of the congregation, but the family was adamant. Their son would come to Sunday services: it was his right, and that's the way it would be. Long story short, the situation escalated to the point where the police actually got involved—and the story became headline news.

There are almost always other, better options.

In some cases, inclusion isn't especially difficult: the child with autism is high functioning and needs only relatively minor accommodations to succeed in a goal of attending religious school, attending worship services, or preparing for and taking part in major rites of passage. By working closely with parents, pastors or volunteers can relatively easily simplify verbal instructions, add visual instructions, provide books on tape or videos, or otherwise make it easier for a child with language-processing difficulties to grasp the content of a lesson. And the same accommodations that teachers make in school are usually appropriate for religious school. These may include allowing kids with autism to sit in the front of the room; assigning a peer buddy; providing a visual schedule; evaluating the space for too-bright lights, too-distracting posters, or other sensory issues; and so forth. Once those accommodations are in place, many kids with high-functioning autism and Asperger syndrome do pretty well in religious school.

In other cases, the child is low-functioning enough that only very specialized, one-on-one experiences are appropriate—and very often those experiences can be made available. In such cases, everyone, parents included, is clear that typical religious education and rites of passage will have to be modified significantly. And it's usually understood that, while people will do their best, it's possible that things just won't work out.

It's the kids in the middle, though—the kids who represent most of the autism spectrum—who present a problem. On the one hand, they may be perfectly capable of taking part in all aspects of religious life if they're appropriately supported and accommodated. On the other hand, accommodation may be complex and difficult to implement. Because churches, synagogues, and mosques are almost entirely managed and staffed by volunteers, it may be very difficult indeed to get those volunteers on board with the idea of inclusion, trained in the processes of inclusion, and supported when inclusion becomes difficult.

Please note that this chapter refers mainly to Catholic, Protestant and Jewish congregations and religious practices. Resources and information for families of Muslim and Hindu faiths, however, are included in the Resource List in Appendix 3 at the end of this book.

What kind of spiritual home will work for you and your child?

I grew up a Unitarian Universalist. UUs are very low key, progressive, and accepting. They even have a special program called "Welcoming Congregations" that is specifically focused on congregational diversity. UUs welcome young and old, gay and straight, all ethnicities, believers and nonbelievers. Yet, with all that acceptance, it became clear very early on that including a child on the autism spectrum would be well-nigh impossible. The reasons weren't philosophical: they were practical.

The UU denomination as a whole is very small. UU Sunday schools are often tiny, and Tom was the only autistic child in the group. Volunteer teachers were uncomfortable working with him, and the church wasn't big enough to have a director of religious education. Sunday school met at the same time as church, which meant I couldn't shadow him unless I intended to avoid church services altogether—which made church membership rather pointless in my view.

We tried simply bringing our son to services, and he was willing to sit and zone out for an hour—but clearly he was getting little from the experience. And while he was physically inside the church building, he was also an anomaly: the kid who just didn't fit in. He wasn't included; he was tolerated. The net outcome of our attempts at religious inclusion was less than ideal.

After much soul-searching and research, I began to understand the problem I was facing. In order to have my son meaningfully included in a UU Sunday school program, I would need to design an appropriate program and then present it myself. That's because the denomination had never been asked to serve people with developmental delays or speech/language challenges; as a result, they had never thought much about how such a program would be implemented.

I may, someday, invent the UU inclusion program. But when my son was little, I was far too busy helping him to be a part of the community to take months out to build a theological curriculum, especially with the knowledge that so few would be likely to make use of it.

What that taught me is that religious-school inclusion for "in-between" kids with autism is really only practical when the religious denomination and the particular setting (church, synagogue, mosque, etc.) are large enough and structured enough to make inclusion practical. That means that inclusion is most practical when you are part of a denomination that has staff, resources, and support available—or when you, the parent, have the time, energy, and ability to work closely with your child and the volunteer members of your religious home.

If those elements aren't present in your congregation of choice, you may need to make compromises, come up with creative solutions, or make significant changes in the way you practice your faith (much more on all these possibilities later in this chapter). You can also tap into some of the many resources that have been created specifically to support inclusion of children and adults with developmental challenges. The bottom line, though, is that you will probably need to do a fair amount of work to make inclusion work in your place of worship.

Of course, for those families whose religious ties are strong and whose congregation is warm and accepting, none of this may be an issue. Your child may simply be welcome because she's your child and you're part of the "family." There may be volunteers lining up to make it possible for your child to be included in every aspect of religious life. Your child may already be an active participant in all aspects of religious life. If that's the case, though, you're probably not reading this chapter!

Finding the right congregation

When you have a child with autism, the nearest house of worship may not be the best choice. In fact, you may even find that the denomination you grew up in just isn't going to work for your child. That's because, as is so often the case, the leadership of the institution and the makeup of the members are in many ways more important than convenience or even your personal inclination.

If you're a Catholic, you probably grew up going to the local parish church. And that might work for your child with autism. Then again, it might not—and you may need to drive a good distance to find a church that accepts and accommodates his needs. If you truly want to be an active and engaged member of a Catholic church, you'll make the drive. And because you made the effort, you'll reap the rewards.

If you grew up a Methodist, you may assume that your family will join the nearest Methodist church—if for no other reason than convenience and tradition. If you grew up a Conservative Jew, you probably planned on joining the nearest Conservative synagogue. But just as Methodist and Presbyterian Protestants have a great deal in common, so do Conservative and Reconstructionist Jews. It may be a better choice for your autistic child—and, thus, for your entire family—to select a different but similar denomination where the whole family is embraced and accepted.

Having said all that, it's also important to note that many churches and synagogues are already taking action to ensure that families like yours are fully supported and included. They may be offering special family services, creating peer-buddy programs, or developing aural and visual teaching aides to help children like yours really understand and engage with religious teachings. They may be opening up vacation Bible school to kids on the autism spectrum or offering special-needs classes to prepare children with autism for confirmation, Bar Mitzvah, and so forth. The problem is that you won't find all that information in the local telephone directory. You may not even find it on the congregational website. You certainly won't find it on the order of service.

So how do you seek out and find that "right" spiritual home?

START LOCAL

While it's possible that your local church or synagogue will be a poor match for your family, it's equally possible that it will be a great match. Of course, it's very important that you—the parents—are comfortable there, so a good first step is simply to attend services with or without your children. Are you comfortable with the preacher, the congregation, the whole "gestalt" of the place? If so, it's time to learn more about the congregation's inclusive practices and options by interviewing the pastor, rabbi, or director of religious education. If not, go on to the next step.

ASK AROUND

Where do other local families with autistic kids go to services? What's working well for their child? There's only one way to find out, and that's to ask. Query your local parent-support group, the other parents in your child's class, and anyone else who might have good local information about supportive, inclusive congregations. If you find a great match through these means, wonderful! If not, go on to the next step.

CONNECT WITH YOUR REGIONAL DENOMINATIONAL OFFICE

Almost every religious denomination is organized into regional districts. Each district has its own leadership. Those district leaders are often terrific resources for information about inclusive congregations. They're very likely to know, for example, that the church two towns to the west has just started a family service specifically intended for families whose kids can't sit still through a typical service. They're also likely to know who the inclusive movers and shakers are in your community—the parents or religious professionals who have taken it upon themselves to promote and support inclusive religious services and educational programs. These are the people who can help you the most because they've made it their business to do so.

USE GOOGLE

By searching for terms like "autism Methodist" or "autism reform Jewish" and the name of your town (or the nearest large town), you may hit upon a jewel. When I tried it myself, I found several congregations that are instituting inclusive Sunday schools, vacation Bible schools, and other autism-friendly programs. Typically, congregations don't make it a point to advertise inclusion—so you really may have to dig. Says Anne Masters, director of Pastoral Ministry with Persons with Disabilities at the Archdiocese of Newark, "Keep Googling! If your expectation is that nothing's being done, you assume nothing has changed. But it is changing! Families aren't getting parish bulletins, so don't know that they're welcome."

Once you find one or more "candidate" houses of worship and have visited on your own, you may want to take the next steps toward having your children included in either worship services or in religious school. Even if your child is high functioning, though,

I do not recommend simply enrolling her in religious school and walking away with your fingers crossed. Your religious home is much more than an activity, and your child's acceptance is meaningful to everyone in your family. Because of this, it's important to start off on the right foot—with trust, communication, and mutual respect.

Say good-bye to your childhood anxieties

If you're like many people, your childhood memories of attending services involve being washed and brushed up until you shone; wearing stiff, uncomfortable clothing; being expected to behave like a lady or gentleman—and hearing about it, loudly, if you didn't. You may not have known the clergy person personally; you may not even have known the names of most of the congregants; and unless you were most unusual, you certainly didn't take an active role in creating or implementing events, programs, or even potlucks.

Now, here you are, having to get hands-on and involved. And with a child on the autism spectrum, you may be feeling doubly anxious.

While anxiety may be understandable, though, it's not helpful. You'll need to be able to get in there and ask questions, offer advice, and even take over if necessary. You may find yourself organizing events, simply because you want to be sure your child is appropriately included. And because your child is autistic, you'll have to be able to handle congregants' questions, concerns, fears, and ignorance with a smile and a sense of humor.

What this means in practical terms is that you'll need to grow a thickish skin. If your child makes a noise and someone frowns, you'll need to find a way to ignore the frown, respond to it with a smile, or otherwise cope with your feelings. You may even, depending on your child's behavior and needs and your inclinations, need to introduce the entire congregation to the issues of autism and inclusion.

It may help to remember that every toddler in the congregation makes noise, every child is occasionally unruly, and many adults are known to be "difficult." Your child may have eccentricities, but it's unlikely that she's more difficult or disruptive than many other children. And it's extremely likely that your child is more innocent and less intentionally rude or mean than the vast majority of children in the congregation. Says Trish Keen, director of religious education at Corpus Christi parish in Landsdowne, Pennsylvania, "Bring your child into the sanctuary. All children need time to learn to behave. People bring toddlers, and they don't have a long attention span, but they learn. My experience is that dirty looks are not for real: they're perceived by the family. Mom was so embarrassed because her child isn't paying attention or is being distracting, but it didn't bother anyone else! Sometimes you can't see the forest for the trees. You're thinking everyone else is noticing; you're very self-conscious."

It may also help to remember that inclusion of children and adults with disabilities and challenges is basic to all religions. Search the books that are basic to your faith, and you will find many passages that guide us to include, support, care for, and accept those with all sorts of challenges. While you may not want to quote scripture to members of your congregation, you can hold those passages in your heart as you do the hard work of helping your child become an active part of his religious community.

On a related note, you may want to know that some people believe that children with autism have a special connection to the divine. While this is by no means a universally held belief, one autistic author, William Stillman, has written two books on the subject. You may find *The Soul of Autism* and *Autism and the God Connection* worth a read.

How to introduce your house of worship to your child with autism, and vice versa

In essence, you'll be introducing your child to your new spiritual home at the same time that you're introducing your spiritual home to your child. That's because so much of your child's success depends upon his feeling comfortable in the space and with the rules of the church, synagogue, or mosque. So while you might meet up once or twice with your new clergy person, director of religious education, or religious education teacher, you're likely to be introducing your child very early on in the process.

Before even getting started, I highly recommend going to http://rwjms.umdnj.edu/boggscenter/products/documents/AutismandFaith.pdf and downloading and printing out several copies of a booklet called *Autism and Faith: A Journey into Community*. This little booklet, the result of a great deal of work on the part of its New Jersey-based authors, is an indispensable resource for families and congregations interested in religious inclusion. While it doesn't cover all the details, it includes wonderful first-person stories, suggestions, tips, and hints from families of many different faiths. It also includes a useful resource section, guidelines for clergy, and more. Keep a copy for yourself, and provide copies to anyone you feel could benefit from its contents.

Next, you'll start preparing your child for inclusion—and your new congregation for your child. There are some basic guidelines for introducing your child with autism to your new place of worship; these are similar to the guidelines you'd use to introduce your child to any new place or situation. The difference, though, is that you may feel that there's more at stake. Another difference is that you'll need to involve members of the congregation or the clergy at each step along the way: their active participation (and, from time to time, permission) will help to move the process forward in a positive way.

USE VIDEO OR PHOTOS TO GIVE YOUR CHILD A TASTE OF WHAT HE WILL ENCOUNTER

Ideally, videotape a service or program that your child will attend. Before videotaping or photographing a service, though, be sure to get permission from the clergy person *and* lay leadership. You may be asked to put a notice in the order of service letting congregants know who you are and what you intend to do; it's also possible that there will be objections to being photographed or videotaped. If objections are raised, of course, you'll need to respect that and either avoid photographing those individuals or only photograph the sanctuary when it's empty.

PROVIDE YOUR CHILD WITH A CLEAR, STEP-BY-STEP PICTORIAL AND/OR WRITTEN GUIDE TO TAKING PART IN SERVICES, EVENTS, OR RELIGIOUS SCHOOL

Of course, you'll need to find out just what will be expected of her, so attending events yourself ahead of time (with a camera, if possible) is key. It's also important to ask the clergy person, director of religious education, or teacher just what the rules are in religious-education programs and what a typical schedule of events looks like.

PRACTICE, PRACTICE, PRACTICE AT HOME

When your child enters the sanctuary, she should know precisely what to do and what to expect—and have mastered the ability to walk in quietly, sit down, say hello, and so forth.

PRACTICE, PRACTICE, PRACTICE IN THE SANCTUARY ITSELF

Stop by on an "off" day when your clergy person is present. Introduce your child. Show her an order of service. Practice coming in and sitting in a pew. Practice standing, sitting, kneeling, singing, and so forth. If you can, ask the clergy person to show your child the different items used during a service. If you intend to allow your child to read, play with toys, etc., during service, check with the pastor to be sure this is acceptable. Then allow your child to practice using her things quietly.

VISIT THE RELIGIOUS-SCHOOL AREA DURING AN OFF HOUR WHEN YOU CAN MEET WITH THE TEACHER

Introduce your child, and allow him to explore the space. Discuss your child's needs, challenges, and abilities with the teacher. Together with the teacher (and/or the director of religious education or clergy person) develop a plan for managing any potential problems. There are often easy ways to circumvent problems (for example, your child will bring a special smock from home; your child will bring a glue stick; you'll provide gluten-free snacks; your child will attend only a portion of the class; you'll help transition your child from the sanctuary to the classroom; and so forth.)

Remember that your child's teacher is a volunteer, and most of the time she has no background or training in special needs. That means that (1) you're the expert when it comes to behavior management and your child, and that (2) the teacher may have real and legitimate concerns and fears about including an autistic child in her class. The more help, support, and resources you can provide, the easier it will be for her to include your child effectively.

DISCUSS AND PLAN FOR WAYS TO INTRODUCE YOUR CHILD TO THE REST OF THE CHILDREN

Will you make a point of explaining his special needs? If so, how will they be presented? Will you ask the class to do anything special?

Is there a child in the class who could act as a peer buddy during transitions or other tricky times?

PREPARE INSTRUCTIONS FOR HANDLING A MELTDOWN

Have a plan in place that allows the teacher easily and quickly to manage a difficult situation without anxiety. That plan, of course, could involve sending a messenger to get you from the sanctuary.

IF YOUR CHILD IS EXPECTED TO WEAR DIFFERENT CLOTHES, BUY THEM EARLY AND HAVE YOUR CHILD WEAR THEM FOR AN HOUR OR MORE ON A REGULAR BASIS

If she can't bear the special clothes, find alternative options that are acceptable.

While all these tips and guidelines should be helpful across denominations, of course, each religious entity has its own traditions, expectations, and resources. With that in mind, take a look at the next sections. You'll find much more specific information available for families of the Catholic, Protestant, and Jewish faiths.

In the Catholic church

The marvelous thing about Catholicism, from the point of view of a family with an autistic child, is that it is practiced in almost the same way week after week, no matter where you are. What that means is that resources created by one Catholic church will be helpful in every Catholic church. It also means that your child with autism should be able to use the same basic set of resources in a variety of different locations (visiting relatives, on vacation, and so forth). Perhaps a bit less marvelous for the child with autism are the smell of incense, the flickering candles, and the requirement that children interested in Confirmation and First Communion attend religious-education classes.

First Communion of Peter Jaskiewicz, with Monsignor Thomas Flanigan (photo by BradleyDigital.com)

Another tricky issue for Catholic families with an autistic child is that, unlike Protestant churches, Catholic churches do not run Sunday school and services concurrently. Children are generally expected to attend Mass and to do so reasonably quietly and attentively. Yes, some churches have special rooms where parents of young children and babies can go if the noise level gets out of hand—but by and large, it's assumed that a child older than two or three will be able to sit through services. If your child or teen simply can't manage to sit for an hour, it may be difficult to attend services as a family at all. Unless, that is, you can find a church where family services are available—something that's becoming increasingly popular overall, not just for families of children with disabilities but also for families in general.

Individual dioceses within the Catholic church have done a great deal to ensure inclusion of children with autism in all aspects of Catholic life. Among other things, they've created picture books to prepare children to sit through the Mass; they've developed educational materials to help youngsters get through CCD classes (Confraternity of Christian Doctrine); and they've come up with accommodations to make Confirmation and First Communion preparation much easier. In fact, as one Catholic educator told me, there's no hard-and-fast rule about just when a child must go through those rites: it's really no problem to delay a year or two.

A list of specific Catholicism and autism websites is included in Appendix 3 at the back of this book. The Archdiocese of Newark and Pittsburgh, in particular, have extensive materials available. If for any reason your individual church tells you your child cannot be confirmed or take communion, it's well worth while to connect, first, with your own archdiocese and then, if necessary, with those archdioceses that have taken a proactive stance toward including children with autism. There's an excellent chance that, with the right support, your child will in fact be able to be included in these sacraments. Still, if your child is nonverbal or otherwise profoundly disabled you may need to connect with someone who has been through the process and can guide you and your family.

Knowing about those resources makes a difference, especially when you're feeling pushed aside by a particular congregation—so does empowering yourself by finding a church that's willing to work with you and not against you. Says one Catholic dad of a young son with autism:

One of our earliest experiences in church was being asked to leave by the usher. John was having a bad day; he was two or three. That was one of the experiences that motivated me to get more involved. In Philadelphia, there's a whole office that deals solely with persons with disabilities. I had gone to Catholic school as a boy, and I assumed that John would go to Catholic school—and we were shocked to hear that "this is not the place for him." That was not a pleasant feeling. I wrote to the director of religious education and explained our situation; John now goes to CCD with an aide from the archdiocese. Teachers are parents and/or teens who don't know how to help him, but the aide was great. He made First Communion; he's been a lector with me. I push him hard to prepare; he gets a shorter reading, and we practice it for a month. People see him up there, and within the parish and his school, they know he's the kid who's not afraid to stand up on the altar and read.

While there is a fairly wide range of resources available to Catholic parents, children, and churches interested in including a person with autism, there's plenty more to be done. If you're a Catholic parent interested in adding to the resources available to help children and adults with autism become full members of the Catholic church, you'll find plenty of opportunities to do so!

In Protestant churches

Protestantism runs such a wide gamut that it's really impossible to create a single set of materials to support children with autism as they attend services and religious school. Of course, there are elements in common: almost every church conducts services on Sunday mornings. Most pass out orders of service as you walk in. Many say the Lord's Prayer, sing hymns, listen to a homily, and make church announcements. But the order in which this is done varies. And, of course, some denominations that could be called Protestant— Unitarians and Quakers, to name two—rarely if ever pray aloud.

This means that if you're joining a Protestant church, you may or may not find specific, premade materials that will introduce your child to the experience of being at that individual church.

What you will find, however, are educational materials focused on key Christian concepts and Bible stories, created specifically for individuals with intellectual disabilities. You'll also find that every major Protestant denomination has created its own set of resources for congregations interested in including individuals with disabilities. In many cases, these resources include not only written materials but also trained professionals able and willing to counsel your individual congregation, clergy person, and director of religious education. (A list of disabilities resources for major Protestant denominations is included in Appendix 3 at the back of this book.)

What the incredible breadth of Protestantism also means is that you are almost certainly going to have to build your own resources relative to the individual church of your choice. That's because it's highly unlikely that any preexisting social story or video will provide your child with a really useful introduction to what to expect, what to do, and what the rules are in your individual house of worship.

In a way, this is a blessing in disguise, though: by sitting through services and religious school with your child's needs in mind, you'll get a very good sense of where pitfalls may lie—and be able to plan accordingly. And when you actually create social stories or videos to help your child prepare for her church experience, you'll have a far better sense of what the service is all about than you might if you simply showed up and sat down in a pew.

As mentioned before, while Protestant churches obviously differ in terms of the details of their teachings, services and polity, there are a great many similarities among denominations. As a result, you may find it spiritually possible to make a shift from one denomination to another if the congregation and pastor are more welcoming and accommodating.

In Judaism

In some ways, if you've visited one synagogue, you've visited one synagogue. Yes, there are many commonalities among Reform, Conservative, Orthodox, and Reconstructionist synagogues, but there are also many differences. The opening of the ark and the reading of the Torah are almost always a part of the service; but the questions of whether a prayer shawl or yarmulke is worn, how the congregation prays, what happens after services, and so forth will vary. Religious education, too, varies widely. What that means to the parent of a child with autism is that do-it-yourself materials may be needed to prepare your child for inclusion at a particular synagogue. Nevertheless, there are plenty of resources available to help you in the process—and there are a wide range of books, videos, and ideas available for simplifying and/or streamlining Torah studies, Shabbat prayers, and the high holidays.

The really wonderful thing about Judaism as it relates to the child with autism is that so much of the experience of being a Jew is centered on the home. What that means is that your child with autism can experience the vast majority of major Jewish events—Shabbat, Passover, Rosh Hashanah, Yom Kippur, Hanukkah, and so forth—without needing to cope with the difficulties of attending services or religious school. Of course, you, the parents, can teach your child a great deal about Judaism without the involvement of a trained rabbi. You can even introduce your child to Jewish music and song, Jewish history, Jewish culture, and Jewish stories—all at a pace and in the style that meets your child's particular needs.

Left to right: David Heiligman, Tyler Zlatin, and Joshua Lai celebrate their Bar Mitzvah together at Congregation Shalom Aleichem in Columbia, MD (photograph by Rabbi Joanne Heiligman)

All that said, though, most families will want their child to be Bar or Bat Mitzvah—and that's where the real challenge comes in. Traditionally, the Bar Mitzvah experience involves reading a Torah portion in Hebrew, speaking from the bema, and essentially running a service. For some children with autism, this is actually a wonderful experience: many children with Asperger syndrome and high-functioning forms of autism have no trouble at all memorizing. And one great plus of autism is that stage fright is rare.

One mom describes her experience with the Bat Mitzvah for her daughter with Asperger syndrome as a real triumph. The family had not been especially involved with religion or Judaism during their daughter's early years; but when it came close to the time for the Bat Mitzvah, they, like many Jewish families, suddenly realized that the ceremony and experience of coming of age were important enough to seek out and find a welcoming synagogue and a tutor willing to work with their child on her Torah portion.

What they found, after a bit of searching, was a Reconstructionist synagogue with an open and welcoming attitude. Most importantly, the synagogue's director of religious education had a child with a developmental disability—and a solid commitment to inclusion. In the long run, not only was the Bat Mitzvah a roaring success, but it turns out that the Bat Mitzvah girl had a real talent for learning and speaking Hebrew. The event itself was tailor-made and included the whole family in a dramatic presentation. And the young girl, now a full member of the congregation, has been tapped to help tutor others in Hebrew reading and pronunciation.

Anna Greenberg's Bat
Mitzvah at Mishkan Shalom

Of course, this is a lovely story and inspiring for those whose autistic children are closer to "quirky" than to disabled. But for the child who has more profound disabilities, the Bar or Bat Mitzvah is a real challenge. It's not, however, a challenge that can't be overcome. To prove that, one father made a movie about the Bar Mitzvah of his son, *Praying with Lior*. While Lior has Down syndrome as opposed to autism, many of the messages of the film are highly relevant. Lior, like many children with autism, seems to have a special connection to the divine. And, like many children with autism, Lior can be difficult to

teach and reach. The video and its supporting website (www.prayingwithlior.com) may be a useful resource. Certainly, the links it provides to Jewish special-education resources will be helpful to many parents and congregations.

Another family was actually able to have their nonverbal son with autism Bar Mitzvah at the age of seventeen. This was an unusual event, but the synagogue involved was willing to create a special program for a small group of young men with similar special needs.

Dov Shestack (third from left)
on Roshashona 2007. Also
pictured: Miriam Shestack
(sister), Portia Iverson (mom),
John Shestack (dad)

What if inclusion doesn't work?

What if, despite all your hard work, your child is just too anxious, loud, disruptive, or different to be included effectively in worship services or religious school? It's probably worth your while to try a few simple, creative measures before just calling it quits. After all, you joined this congregation because it was important to you, and it's likely that you have strong feelings about your autistic child's becoming a full and included member of a faith community.

PLAY DETECTIVE

Often, a child with autism will behave badly for a very good reason. That reason, though, may be hard to detect. With the help of others involved with your child's religious education, keep careful notes. When does your child act out? What are the most difficult moments? Can you detect a pattern? It's perfectly possible that your child's outbursts or tears are caused by something predictable and preventable—such as a door alarm, the smell of a particular craft material, or a classmate who delights in poking him. If that's the case, you can fix the problem and move on.

SLOW IT DOWN

Consider the possibility that several hours in a religious setting may be too much for your child, but a few minutes may be just right. Perhaps your child can join you in the sanctuary for the first few minutes of the service or take part in selected portions of religious education (selected with the help of her teacher or clergy person).

TAKE A BREAK

Your child may not be ready to take part in formal religious services and programs. It's okay to take some time off and try again in a few months or even a year.

TRADE OFF

If you and your partner or spouse are serious about wanting a spiritual home, you can trade off time in the sanctuary and time with your autistic child. You may want to stay home with your child, shadow her in the classroom, or support her in the sanctuary—but whoever's "on" for the week must cope when things get out of hand.

TRY ANOTHER SETTING

If all else fails, the problem may be with the setting. Sometimes, the religious home that's perfect for you just isn't a good fit for your child. If that's the case, you may want to consider exploring more options before giving up altogether.

Top tips for religious inclusion

- Be flexible. The nearest or most obvious choice of church or synagogue may not be the most welcoming to your child with autism.

- Ask! No matter what your religious affiliation, it's well worth your time to ask locally and regionally about special programs, services, accommodations, or supports. It's quite possible that they're available but not widely publicized.

- Use available resources. In many cases, there are resources—written and human—available to smooth the path to inclusion. Use them!

- Communicate. Know that most clergy and volunteers really do want to include your child, but they may be nervous or simply unaware of what autism is and how to help. It's up to you to be sure the lines of communication are wide open. Let the people who work with your child know how he learns and provide resources as necessary.

- Practice makes perfect. Use photos or videos to prepare your child for inclusion, and practice over and over again at home and in your house of worship, so that your child is truly ready for inclusion.

- Be willing to change. If your child simply isn't ready, be prepared to step back from your goal of full inclusion for the time being. Try taking part in only small portions of the service, shadowing your child, or homeschooling some of the religious content you want your child to learn.

Tip sheet

On the next pages is a tip sheet that you should copy and share with clergy and volunteers in your church, synagogue, or mosque who will be working with your child or other children on the autism spectrum.

✓

Tip sheet for welcoming kids and teens with autism to your house of worship

Congratulations! You have a new member of your congregation who is going to gain tremendously from his or her involvement in your community. As someone who will be interacting with this young person and his or her family, your enthusiastic and creative support will make all the difference—not only to the young person but also to the family and even the congregation as a whole.

As you develop your plans for inclusion, be sure to tap into existing denominational resources. No matter what your religious affiliation, there are people, materials, and models you can tap into to help you include a family with special needs. In addition, these tips may help you get started:

1. Know that every autistic child is unique. If you've met or worked with an autistic child in the past, it's very possible that your new community member will surprise you.

2. Find out about your new congregant and his family. Ask his parents for any useful information they can provide about his special challenges and abilities. Be sure to ask about his past experiences with and knowledge of religious services and education—kids with autism may have fewer experiences with attending worship services than their typical peers.

3. If your new congregant can tell you about herself, be sure to ask her whether she has any specific concerns or anxieties.

4. Start with the basics. Instead of assuming that the child with autism already knows the rules, expectations, stories, and traditions of your denomination, assume that he doesn't. The truth is that other children in the congregation may also be able to use a refresher in the basics.

5. Use visual and hands-on teaching tools. You may be used to telling kids what they need to know, but kids with autism may have a tough time with verbal instructions. You can demonstrate, write down your instructions, or even offer hand-over-hand help so that your congregant with autism really "gets" your message.

6. Give direct instructions. Some children can accurately guess what's coming next or where you're headed when you line up at the door. Kids with autism don't. You'll need to be very direct in telling your congregant with autism where to go, what to do, and when to do it. You may need to provide reminders to help her stay focused.

7. Be aware of possible sensory issues. Kids with autism may have unusual concerns about smells, loud noises, or physical sensations. Of course, you can't change your entire religious service or curriculum; but, for example, in a religious-education class, sticky paste can be replaced with a glue stick, dangling mobiles can be put away, and the class as a whole can be asked to keep the noise level down to a dull roar.

8. Use other young congregants as peer buddies. Most parishes, synagogues, or mosques include at least a few kids who are good at and enjoy helping others. As you can, team your autistic congregant up with a buddy who's willing to lend a helping hand. During breaks, the buddy or buddies can spend a little extra time just hanging out with the autistic child.

9. Use your autistic congregant's parents as aides. It's quite possible that your autistic member will need extra help in adjusting to your routine or handling the expectations of your community. If you have the time and inclination, you can certainly work with him. But it's absolutely fine to ask his mom or dad to help out when necessary or to let his parents know what skills to work on.

10. Don't lower your expectations. It's tempting to allow a child with autism to do his own thing, especially if he's quiet while he does so. But unless you run into serious behavior issues (which you should address with the child's parents), it's important to find a way to include your autistic congregant in religious education and worship.

Chapter 8

The Visual and Performing Arts

There's a strange myth out there that people with autism have no emotions. The myth may have developed as a result of Dustin Hoffman's deadpan presentation of an autistic man in the movie *Rain Man*, or it may be an outcome of the fact that kids with autism often express their feelings idiosyncratically. Whatever the reasons, it's simply not true. In fact, some people with autism are among the most passionate, expressive individuals in the world.

All too often, though, people with autism receive far too few opportunities to express their emotions. Most are limited in their verbal skills, and, of course, "acting out" is frowned on. In theory, the obvious solution is to provide kids with autism with plenty of opportunities to express themselves through the arts. Unfortunately, opportunities for artistic expression are increasingly rare. In fact, even for typical kids, the arts are considered "extras"; and as a result, many schools are losing their art, music, and drama programs.

Since art, music, and performance are the most basic of all human forms of expression, this is not just a sad fact—for kids in general, and for kids with autism in particular, it's a terrible loss. Fortunately, it's easy enough for families to fill the artistic void and to open up creative avenues of expression for children who may find verbal communication to be cumbersome, confusing, or even impossible.

It's also important to note that the visual and performing arts may well be areas in which a person with autism may be not only competent but may also be extraordinarily talented. Rumors abound that Mozart may have been autistic; certainly, the "artistic temperament" and autism have a lot in common. One website suggests that Vincent Van Gogh, Ludwig Beethoven, Gustav Mahler, and Richard Strauss may have been diagnosable with autism. Movie actor and musician Dan Ackroyd has mentioned being diagnosed with Asperger syndrome. All these people were or are intense, passionate, and extraordinarily talented. They were or are also very (sometimes even extremely) idiosyncratic in their relationships, their behavior, and their temperament.

Could your autistic child be the next Mozart or Van Gogh (minus the ear issue)? There's only one way to find out, and that's to expose your child to opportunities that allow him to explore his artistic abilities.

What are the arts, and why do they matter?

The visual arts include painting, sculpture, photography, videography, drawing, printing, and—depending on your point of view—crafts such as pottery, weaving, paper sculpture, jewelry making, and so forth. For children and teens, "art" is generally understood to mean the hands-on creation of visual works in a variety of mediums based either on the child's own imagination or on models provided by teachers. It may also mean instruction in or exploration of fine art and art history: strolling through art galleries, visiting sculpture gardens, watching videos, or reading books about art, and so forth.

The performing arts are generally understood to mean music (voice, instrumental, synthesized, including every genre from gangsta rap to Wagnerian opera), drama (theatrical performances of any kind in person or on film or video, along with improvisation, talent shows, etc.), and dance (again, any kind—tap, ballet, hip hop, zumba, ballroom, you name it). Under that same umbrella of performing arts fall puppet shows, circuses, Siegfried and Roy, the Cirque du Soleil, magic shows…

In other words, the arts cover a lot of ground. In fact, it's very hard to live in the wider world without becoming—in some way—a patron of the arts. If your child with autism has never been to the movies, attended a show or concert, watched a juggler or magician, or at the very least seen a puppet show, she has lived a limited life indeed. Of course, there are often concerns with taking autistic kids into very large, crowded places where good behavior is not only preferred but required—but The Wiggles (a beloved Australian children's performing group) don't really expect kids to sit down and be good. And small, informal events may be presented at schools, festivals, churches—in fact, all over the community. Many such events are brief and informal, and quite a few actually encourage kids to get up and move.

Being an audience member or observer of the arts, though, is just the beginning. Kids and teens with autism are often very interested in and even talented in one or another area of the arts. Music, in particular, is an area in which many people on the autism spectrum truly excel (though there are now quite a few celebrated autistic painters and sculptors). And the arts are often used as a therapeutic tool to help kids with speech and communications challenges to connect with others, learn social and speech skills, and connect more fully with their own bodies. There are trained arts therapists in music, art, dance, and drama—and the experience of taking part in the arts can be therapeutic even if it's not presented as therapy *per se.*

How the arts can open the world

For our son, the visual and performing arts have been a tremendous entrée into the wider community. The truth is that Tom's not much of a visual artist, though he does enjoy drawing, sculpting, and other forms of arts and crafts. But even at age eight, he was already a true patron of the arts.

Tom's first trips to the Philadelphia Art Museum, let me be clear, were a disaster. He climbed on benches—a huge no-no—and ran through the galleries. In fact, he behaved very badly, and while we weren't actually asked to leave, the guards' faces made it clear that we were *Not Welcome.*

Within a few years, though, Tom's attitude and level of interest had changed radically. For this, I have to credit an animated television show. The show is called *Little Einsteins,* and it has nothing to do with Albert Einstein and everything to do with introducing children to the arts. Each episode of the program introduces one painting/artist and one piece of classical music/composer, in the context of a really silly story that has nothing whatever to do with either piece of art.

The outcome of watching (and essentially memorizing) these shows, for Tom, was extraordinary. His familiarity with the shows led to an interest in recognizing both the music and the paintings.

Imagine our delight and pride when Tom, then about seven-years-old, recognized and rushed to admire Picasso's *Three Musicians* in the contemporary gallery of a major art museum. Tom's dad absolutely beamed as he described the faces of adult museum goers as they watched the little boy's face light up with delight in a work of art. The same thing happened in the Impressionist gallery where Tom recognized Monet's *Water Lilies* and Van Gogh's *Starry Night*. From that moment forward, Tom was hooked on fine art. Unlike other kids his age (or most boys, period), he has a tremendous interest in exploring and experiencing the galleries of art museums.

At age 11, we took him to the Metropolitan Museum of Art in New York, where we took part in a special-needs tour of the museum. The tour—like all educational tours in that museum—included a point during which members of the group stopped and sketched from major works of art. It was then that we discovered that Tom, while not much good at handwriting or even freehand drawing, was actually quite capable of copying and rendering. Who knew?

Little Einsteins and Disney's *Fantasia* also opened the doors to classical music. Like many people with autism, Tom has a remarkable visual and aural memory: he could actually listen to a work from *Fantasia* and tell us exactly what would be happening on screen if we were watching the film. Because of his obvious interest in music (and his delight in picking out chords and scales on the piano), we started him on clarinet and piano lessons at age seven (more on that later in the chapter). Soon, we were taking him to the renowned Family Concerts presented by the Philadelphia Symphony Orchestra, where he not only enjoyed the music but also learned how to comport himself in a high-end cultural venue.

Over time, Tom has taken part in many different musical ensembles and band camp. He has been to plays, concerts, magic shows, circuses, and talent shows. He has performed at recitals and helped to paint theatrical sets. We've also experimented with music and dance therapies.

Tom, to be honest, is no virtuoso. But he has discovered, through the arts, a whole range of interests, talents, and abilities that would never have been open to him if he'd remained stuck in the "box" of autism. Through music, he's developing fine-motor and math skills and the ability to work in cooperation with a group. Through the visual arts, he's learning to discern and create patterns and understand color, shape, and relationships in a sophisticated way. Even better, he has connected with musicians—including other children, teachers, and band directors—who would never have known he existed if he'd remained in the "autism-only" room at school. Will he, someday, be ready to audition for a regional youth orchestra? Like any parents, we push the practicing and keep our fingers crossed.

If it takes a village to raise a child, then the people who are helping Tom to cultivate his musical talent and interests are a part of that village. And if the arts are a central part of what it means to be human, then Tom is becoming more and more fully actualized as a human being as a result of his involvement with the arts.

Painting, sculpting, drawing, crafting, and your child with autism

The visual arts are all about self-expression, something that's important to everyone but particularly important to a child whose social and verbal skills are compromised. And children and teens with autism who may have few overt communication skills may discover they have a real fascination and/or talent for self-expression through the visual arts. (In Appendix 3, I've listed a few online galleries where the work of talented autistic artists is displayed.) What's more, since people with autism are often visual learners with a great talent for

observation of fine detail, there's a real opportunity in the visual arts to find and build on special strengths. Many websites, organizations, and even galleries offer opportunities for people with autism to exhibit their work—though, of course, it's not necessary to stick with the autism community when putting your child's artwork on display.

Alex, age 10, at Cartooning Camp held at Acting Antics, in partnership with Young Rembrants Program through the Center on Central in Paoli, PA

Most kids are exposed to the visual arts early in life, and it's quite possible that your child with autism was asked to cut, draw, paint, or paste as a little one. It's also quite possible that she had a tough time with the visual arts—not because of a lack of interest in the arts themselves but because the tools generally introduced to toddlers and preschoolers are notoriously difficult for children with autism. Scissors require advanced fine-motor skills that may be delayed in an autistic child. Finger paints, gooey play dough, sticky paste, and smelly clay all present significant sensory challenges. Even markers may have a strong smell. All these issues may have turned your child away from visual self-expression. But the reality is that there are many different kinds of visual media and many ways to accommodate sensory challenges.

When Tom was a toddler (and even now), he had a difficult time with correctly grasping pencils, crayons, and other slim objects. And while he could observe and recall visual images perfectly, he had a hard time reproducing them. Nevertheless, he adored drawing (still does). To help him build on his interests while accommodating his challenges, we actually bought oversized paper and taped it to the walls at toddler height. Then we handed him colorful, water-based (smell-free) markers. Tom spent many a happy afternoon creating free-form murals all around the living room!

Art therapy, art class, or...?

According to the American Art Therapy Association:

> Art therapy is a mental health profession that uses the creative process of art making to improve and enhance the physical, mental and emotional well-being of individuals of all ages. It is based on the belief that the creative process involved in artistic self-expression helps people to resolve conflicts and problems, develop interpersonal skills, manage behavior, reduce stress, increase self-esteem and self-awareness, and achieve insight.

If you have a child with autism, chances are all this looks like a good match for your child's needs. In fact, children with autism really can thrive in a good art-therapy program. Unlike many types of therapy, too, art therapy actually builds skills while it also provides therapeutic services. These facts suggest that it might be well worthwhile to involve your child with autism in an art-therapy program.

There are, however, a few drawbacks to art therapy as opposed to simple exposure to the arts, an art class, or an art-studio experience. The first, as is often the case, is money. Virtually no insurance program will pay for any type of art therapy, so if you choose that route, you're on your own (unless you're able to get a grant to support an art-therapy program in your community). Of course, art therapy costs more than most ordinary kids' art classes because it's a professional therapeutic program—and because therapy is generally offered one-on-one or in a very small group.

Another drawback to art therapy is the reality that there is no opportunity to move easily from therapy to skill building or into a community arts program. In fact, a child who starts his art experience in therapy will actually have to leave his therapist (and all the connections he has built) in order to try out an ordinary kids' painting class. There are a few exceptions to that rule: some community arts centers do employ art therapists, and some art therapists also teach ordinary art classes. But overall, art therapy is *therapy*, while classes or arts-related programs in the community are intended to be opportunities to get out, explore, and have fun.

Bottom line: arts therapy can be a great way for your child to discover new ways to communicate and express himself. But it's unlikely to be a good entrée into the larger community. If your child is really unable to take part in a general arts program, it's a good way to dip his toes into the world of visual arts in a safe, supportive setting. If your child is able, though, to take part in a community arts program—even with your hands-over-hand support—you might want to consider the community option.

In addition to art therapy, there are special-needs arts programs that may be of interest to you and your child. VSA Arts is an international arts organization that states on its website, "We were founded on one belief—that the arts belong to everyone and everyone deserves equal access." With that in mind, the program offers a wide range of educational programs, exhibitions, and opportunities for artists with special needs to exhibit their work. Its focus is on inclusion, which means that VSA Arts makes the arts accessible to everyone, regardless of ability, talent, or economic status. Several other such groups reach out and provide supported arts programs to children and adults with disabilities. I've listed some of these organizations in Appendix 3.

Getting started with the visual arts

By far, the simplest way to help your child begin to explore the visual arts is at home—with your help and support. You don't need to be "artistic" to explore arts materials with your child. In fact, if you're less bound to artistic conventions and more willing to experiment with and/or alongside your child, you may have a lot more fun. Bear in mind that you're not teaching an art class: you're exploring and having fun with (or at least near) your child or children.

A great place for you to prepare for at-home art explorations is at your nearest arts-and-crafts supplies store. If you've never been to one, go! You'll discover an incredible range of materials, techniques, and supplies that you may never have imagined—glitter pens; foam core; feathers; sequins; paints with built-in brushes; clays that can bend; sand painting and mosaic kits; and foamy, air-drying clays that can be colored with markers. Even if your child never gets excited about the visual arts, you may discover a whole new direction for yourself. Naturally, if your child or children can handle themselves in an arts-and-crafts store, they should come along and make their own selections (with some guidance from you, relative to cost and pragmatic concerns).

When you select materials and space for yourself and your child, be aware of your child's interests, abilities, and limits. You obviously don't want an open bottle of poster paint to sit at the elbow of a child with impulsivity issues. In fact, you may not want to work with poster paint at all, given that you can choose crayons, pastels, colored pencils, and other materials that are far less likely to ruin your rug. And if your child with autism reacts badly to slimy textures, you'll want to stay away from certain types of clay, glue, and papier-mâché.

All that said, if you're not sure what your child will or won't like, try not to make too many assumptions. While many kids with autism do react badly to strong smells, sticky materials, difficult-to-manage tools, and so forth, your child may be the exception to that rule. What's more, while some children with autism simply can't and/or won't follow instructions or models, others absolutely love to follow a clear set of rules to a predictable end. Because you don't yet know your child's artistic temperament, you may want to offer a number of options—from "color-by-number" and "build-by-blueprint" kits to open-ended but enticing colors, textures, and materials. Don't spend a fortune—basic, cheap supplies are fine (though if your child is likely to put things in her mouth, you'll want to check that everything is nontoxic).

Some kids will immediately set to work playing with or creating with their art supplies. Others will draw or doodle for a moment and leave the table. Still others will try materials and get frustrated quickly. If your child is among those who don't immediately focus in on art supplies, there are a few strategies you may want to try.

WALK AWAY
Just leave the supplies available, and allow your child to explore them in his own time and in his own way. If, after several days, he doesn't explore them, you may want to move on to the next strategy.

SELECT MATERIALS YOUR CHILD WILL LOVE OR LET HIM SELECT THEM HIMSELF
For years (and even now), Tom loved to pick up bits of colorful litter from the ground. We discovered we could "co-opt" this bad habit by having him specifically collect colored plastic that we then sorted into bins. In the long run, we created a "trash flag" of the United States, which won second prize at a county fair!

MODEL USE OF THE MATERIALS
Some kids with autism don't instantly see or grasp the purpose of art materials. If you model their use by drawing, painting, decoupaging, scrapbooking, etc., your child may become more interested. As you model, talk through what you're doing ("I have a rubber stamp that shows an elephant. I'm going to squish it onto this ink pad"—squish—"and then squish it down on my paper"—squish—"and it makes a picture!") If your child is intrigued, set the materials aside for her to try.

MAKE SOMETHING YOUR CHILD WILL LOVE
When trying to engage Tom, I found that hand puppets were sometimes more effective than I was. So I'd make a paper-bag puppet,

and the puppet and Tom would get chatting. In the long run, Tom was intrigued enough that he decided to make his own puppets. Of course, I had paper bags, yarn, googly eyes, markers, and glue immediately available!

USE VIDEOS TO DEMONSTRATE PROJECTS AND METHODS

Sometimes kids with autism get more interested in almost anything when it's presented on television. Find videos, YouTube Web videos, or children's TV shows with segments on how to use arts materials (check Appendix 3 for ideas). Watch with your child, and have the materials available if she wants to try the activity herself.

USE VIDEOS AND BOOKS TO INTRODUCE YOUR CHILD TO ART HISTORY

When Tom was twelve, he got into Impressionism. He'd seen a few paintings on television (on the show *Little Einsteins*, as I've mentioned) and recognized the paintings on several library books about Monet and Van Gogh. On the basis of that interest, we rented videos about the artists, and I found a book that showed "how to paint like the Impressionists." We didn't create any masterpieces, but we had a lot of fun—and learned more than we ever wanted to know about the Impressionists' private lives!

Creating visual arts in the community

In fact, there's no absolute requirement to get out of your own home in order to learn about, practice, or even exhibit visual arts. But this book is all about getting out, and the fact is that you can find wonderful ideas, insights, and opportunities by getting out and exploring the world of the visual arts. Many towns have art classes available for children; these may be offered through an arts guild, through individual artists, at the library, at an extension school, or even at the local college or university.

If your child is very young (under age six) and seems to enjoy the visual arts, there's no good reason to avoid typical arts classes— assuming you're willing to sit in and intervene if an issue does come up. Most classes for young children are specifically intended to inspire creativity—which means your child's ability to grasp a pencil, listen to verbal instruction, or even talk may be completely unimportant. What really matters is that your child feels at home with the smells, lights, and set-up of the space and that the instructor and other children are congenial.

For older children, the selection of a visual-art class may be a bit trickier. The key, though, is to select a class that's likely to fit your child's interests, abilities, patience level, and sensory profile.

Finding that right class isn't as hard as it sounds. In fact, it's pretty simple. Typical children's arts classes, for example, include drawing, painting, comic-book making, book making, clay sculpture, junk sculpture, paper making, paper sculpture and pop-ups, papier-mâché, printing with fruits and vegetables, watercolor, photography, and even fashion design.

The descriptions for each class are quite specific, and it's easy enough to interpret their significance. For example, "we will experiment with" means kids will have a fair amount of freedom to try out different tools, media, etc. "We will learn to" implies that there will be instruction and right/wrong approaches to an artistic technique. "Have messy fun" means just what it says: goop, stickiness, and mess.

Based on these descriptions, you can make a good guess that "learn the proper way to use a digital camera" isn't going to fly for your free-form autistic teen—but "experiment with a variety of two- and three-dimensional media" might be a great match. Obviously, if you have an autistic teen who is capable of handling a class on the uses of a digital camera, she can tell you which art class (if any) is right for her.

Before signing your child up, talk with the teacher. Artists as teachers can be wonderful role models—but they can also find it very frustrating to have an autistic child in their group. Even if you don't use the word *autistic*, make it clear to the teacher that your child, for example, is interested in photography but may need to have instructions repeated more than once. If you have concerns about the media (e.g., your child will get very anxious if confronted with the need to get her hands gooey), share them. If the teacher responds with uncertain anxiety ("well, we *do* use gooey materials, so I'm not sure what to tell you"), steer clear. If, on the other hand, the teacher is full of ideas for engaging your child based on his needs and interests ("we could substitute clay for papier-mâché when it's time to cover the armature, and I'll show him how to do that. It's a lot less goopy, and it works just as well")—you've found a winner!

Bear in mind that, even with an older child or a child with Asperger syndrome, you may need to be present during at least some of the classes. That's because instructors may give rapid-fire instructions or expect class members to have advanced manual dexterity. Most ten-year-olds can quickly and efficiently tie a knot when so instructed, but your child with autism may have motor delays that make knot-tying very frustrating and difficult. If that's the case, you can step in unobtrusively and just give your child a hand with trickier elements of a project. Over time, your child may be able to build those skills at home and then transfer them to the art-class setting.

A word of warning: beware the preprepared, "quick-and-easy" craft workshops that have become so prevalent. Often, "make your own kite," "make your own puppet," and similar workshops are a lot less quick and easy than they appear to be. Kids have very little time or space for experimentation or even for taking their time to create. As a result, the experience can be very frustrating—not only for your child but for you as well.

Tom Cook on a homeschool field trip, trying out a hand loom at a private studio in Bourne, MA

Advice on visual arts and autism from Donna Williams

Donna Williams was born in Australia in 1963. She is diagnosed with autism and became an international author, artist, singer-songwriter, and screenwriter, as well as a qualified teacher, public speaker, and autism consultant. I asked her to offer advice to parents with autistic children who may have an interest in the visual arts.

> *Lisa*: My child/teen with autism may have a terrific talent in the visual arts. What's the best way to nurture it?

> *Donna*: Depends on the child. If they have severe exposure anxiety [fear of being in the company of others], then you'd do best to leave art materials for discovery and leave them to

it; and when you do discover their work, don't do gush and fuss about it, let it be part of a sacred private experience of self expression and don't go waving it about like a mad puppy.

I also think video and Internet education has huge potential for autistic artists with language-processing or visual–perceptual disorders or exposure anxiety who may be locked out of learning arts in more directly confrontational interactions.

Lisa: Should I sign my child up for art therapy or an art class— or just provide materials and let her go?

Donna: If it's someone with exposure anxiety, it's the latter. If it's someone who copes fine with praise, attention, admiration and is a social learner, then a class may work, provided it is sensorily tolerable.

Lisa: Do I need to let an art teacher know my child has "special needs?"

Donna: Some people just see *people*. Others see "abnormality" or need labels before they can "forgive" "abnormality." I really like the first lot. But you can let them know as an aside, "Oh, by the way, my child has some challenges…" but do define what you mean. So in my case, it'd be, "Oh, by the way, I am partially meaning-deaf, I'm fairly context-blind, I'm face-blind, and I can't consistently hold a simultaneous sense of self and other, and these things contribute to my exposure anxiety, so if I seem a bit odd, it might be some of those things. Oh, and I have some bipolar, OCD, and tics which are medicated, but sometimes my tics might fly out, so just ignore them." And it's about the tone you say it in, too. I say it an everyday way, and I think that helps them know it's really not a big deal, just my "normal" life. And sometimes I don't tell until I need to.

Lisa: What are some of the issues I should be aware of (for example, sensory issues, need to finish a project, etc.)?

Donna: Fans (for those with auditory-verbal agnosia); bright, overhead fluorescents (for those with visual–perceptual disorders); people talking too fast or not checking you've understood what they've said or shown you; allergies and food intolerances... It's going to be individual, and each person needs to have a rough map of their needs and why.

Lisa: How do I talk to the school or extracurricular art instructor about sensory issues with goopy materials, difficulties with scissors, etc.? Are there less gooey alternatives to things like papier-mâché?

Donna: I think it's about the goal, and if the same goal can be met through different means, then why not? So it shouldn't matter if one makes a clay horse, a cardboard horse or a papier-mâché one. It comes down to the teachers. Are they normality conformists? Then, they need to get a little less hung up—actually, a lot less. But, equally, kids with sensory hypersensitivities and phobias also need to reality-test these in small doses and not just cop out.

Lisa: Are there good ways to get my child's artwork out there and on display?

Donna: Yep, there's Saatchi Gallery online, loads of online galleries. You can do your own via MySpace, on a Facebook page, via a www.wordpress.com blog, and you can link works to a PayPal facility to receive payments for them.

But also list where they could be displayed and present them professionally. Email those on the list and ask to show the works there, offer to use a percentage of sales as a fundraiser. So, for example, my art prints and art cards earn 30 percent to the charities and groups which sell them, and I sell art works at reduced rates to some groups so they can auction them as fundraisers.

Sharing your child's artistic creations in the community (showing work and visiting galleries)

If you think your child with autism is too young, too untalented, or in any way not good enough to show off her work in a public space, think again. There are many, many ways for your child to exhibit her creations publicly—assuming she wants to or, at the very least, doesn't object to your doing so.

Similarly, even if your child with autism can't comfortably manage a day at a major art museum, he is almost certainly capable of visiting an exhibit of fine art. That's thanks to the practice of placing fine art in ordinary stores, restaurants, coffee shops, and a wide variety of public spaces, and thanks, too, to the Internet.

In fact, if you and your child are interested in showing or discovering fine art, you'll find that your biggest challenges lie in deciding which of many possible venues to explore first.

Showing off your child's fine art

There are a few major questions to ask when it comes to showing off your child's artistic work:

1. Is your child comfortable with having her work shown publicly, and if so, how publicly?

2. Is your child serious about her work, or is she simply enjoying the experience of expressing herself?

3. Do you want your child's work to be displayed in the context of his autism or on its own merits?

4. Does your child want to sell her work?

5. Is your child truly talented? Be honest with yourself and/or ask others to help you determine whether your child is gifted. That is, is there a real possibility that she will study art and/or become a professional artist?

These questions are important because, first and foremost, artwork belongs to the artist. Even if your child is a brilliant artist, she is under no obligation to show her work. Of course, as a parent, you may want to be sure that certain individuals do see your child's work (grandma, a therapist, a potential art teacher)—but that's quite different from insisting that your child's work be made public.

If your child is truly talented and/or is very serious about his work, you'll want to think carefully about how and where to show it. After all, there is always the possibility that your child will decide to follow his talent toward a degree or even a career in fine art: he certainly wouldn't be the first person with autism to do so. If that's the case, then showing his work in an "autism gallery" may not be an ideal choice (at least to start).

A few congenial places to show your child's art might include the following (from most private to most public):

- The fridge. Displaying your child's work on your refrigerator (or grandma's fridge) makes it clear to your child that you're proud of his work—and he can see evidence of that every day. If he has done something really spectacular, consider framing and hanging it in a place of honor.

- The art studio where he takes his class. If your child is proud of a work of art and the teacher doesn't automatically put it up on the wall, ask her to do so.

- School. Lots of art teachers are willing to put up a child's work in the halls, even if it wasn't created at school.

- A local coffee shop. Many local shops are willing to hang the work of local artists. Of course, once you leave the nonjudgmental sanctity of home and school, you need to know that your child's work is really, truly good. You'll also need to frame and label it.

- A local art show or fair. We entered our kids' work at the local county fair and (like every child who entered) they won ribbons! Tom's "junk flag" won second prize, and this year's "sculpture of Mowgli" won third.

- Online galleries. There are now a number of online galleries where young people with and without disabilities can show off their work. There are a few Web addresses in Appendix 3 of this book; of course, you can also create your own gallery online to share with personal friends and family.

Discovering and viewing fine art

As I mentioned earlier in this book (and in this chapter), our son Tom is a natural museumgoer. But art museums are typically very tough on kids in general—and on kids with autism in general. Patrons don't appreciate noise, there's absolutely *no touching*, and climbing is forbidden. If you don't feel your child is ready for an art museum, though, he may well be ready for a sculpture garden, public art installations, a children's art exhibit, a local gallery, or a show at your local coffee shop. At the very least, you can share picture books of fine art with your child until you feel he's ready to get out and explore.

Sculpture gardens and public art are a great way to introduce a child to fine art. In some places, the art is interactive, too. We've had a fine time trying out sound sculptures, exploring climbable sculptures, and interacting with computer-based sculptures. We've also simply explored and enjoyed sculptures at universities, libraries, and other public institutions. I've listed a few major sculpture gardens in Appendix 3, but to find something local, you can always search the Internet.

Small, local galleries may be a good option for art gazing, particularly if the artist is a friend or the artwork itself is of special interest (showing a local scene or favorite subject). Do be wary, though, if your child is likely to grab, poke, or otherwise behave oddly: artists are, reasonably enough, very protective of their work.

And what could be a better way to be introduced to fine art than in a friendly, neighborhood coffee shop while munching a cookie? These days, Starbucks and other chains (as well as stand-alone local shops) very often show and sell local artists' work. By simply calling your child's attention to the paintings on the wall, you're making her aware of original fine art as a part of her world.

The performing arts and your child with autism

Of all the topics addressed in this book, the performing arts are among the most likely to provide your autistic child with a lifelong skill, a group of friends (or at least associates), and a very, very full schedule. In fact, if your child gets serious about the performing arts, your own life may well become very, very busy (even busier than it is now, if you can imagine that!). And it's not unusual for children with autism to be quite talented, capable, and accomplished in the areas of music and drama.

As with the visual arts, you can introduce your child to the performing arts as a participant or a patron. And, as with the fine arts, you can begin your explorations at home, in a therapeutic setting, in a special-needs setting, or in a typical setting. If your child has a real ability and/or interest in music, I recommend that you consider real lessons as opposed to music therapy (more on this later). Drama and dance, however, are a bit trickier for most kids with autism—and you may want to consider more specialized settings, at least at first.

As an aside, I've found that children with autism have a huge advantage over typical children when it comes to the performing arts. With few exceptions, kids with autism are far less concerned with peer judgments or potential embarrassment than the average child—and as a result, they suffer far less than typical children from stage fright. Our Tom has never had an issue with climbing up on stage and doing his best—nor have most of the autistic performers I know. Since stage fright can get between most people and their best performance, it's great to know that your child may never need to face or overcome this particular issue.

Therapy and the performing arts

If your child has an apparent interest or ability in the area of music, dance, or drama, you may want to build on that interest through therapy. Indeed, the performing arts are a terrific foundation on which to build the skills autistic children need most: body awareness, communication, collaboration, and self-confidence. In general, it's much easier to find programs in music therapy than in dance or drama therapy for children with autism—but all are available in major metropolitan areas, and each has its benefits.

MUSIC THERAPY

The American Music Therapy Association has an entire fact sheet about autism-spectrum disorders on its website, and its claims for the efficacy of music therapy for children with autism are backed up by quite a bit of research. Here's just some of what the AMTA says music therapy can do for your child:

1. Music is considered a "universal language" which provides bridges in a nonthreatening setting between people and/ or between individuals and their environment, facilitating relationships, learning, self-expression, and communication.

2. Music therapy can enable those without language to communicate, participate, and express themselves nonverbally. Very often, music therapy also assists in the development of verbal

communication, speech, and language skills. The interpersonal timing and reciprocity in shared play, turn-taking, listening, and responding to another person are augmented in music therapy with children and adults with autism to accommodate and address their styles of communication.

3. Music therapy allows individuals with diagnoses on the autism spectrum the opportunity to develop identification and appropriate expression of their emotions.

4. Because music is processed in both hemispheres of the brain, music can stimulate cognitive functioning and may be used for remediation of some speech/language skills.

5. Music provides concrete, multisensory stimulation (auditory, visual, and tactile). The rhythmic component of music is very organizing for the sensory systems of individuals diagnosed with autism. As a result, auditory processing and other sensory-motor, perceptual/motor, gross- and fine motor skills can be enhanced through music therapy.

In addition to being generally available, not terribly expensive, and often very attractive to children with autism, music therapy is the best-researched form of arts therapy available. In fact, there are quite a few studies that show music therapy to be a truly effective technique for building many of the skills described above.

I will mention here, however, that music therapy is not the same thing as musical instruction. If your child with autism enjoys playing with, swaying with, and listening to music, music therapy may be a terrific option. If, on the other hand, they seem to show an interest in or talent for making music, I highly recommend that you consider instrumental or vocal instruction either in lieu of or in addition to music therapy. If your child really does have the talent to proceed with music in an inclusive setting, music therapy can't provide him with the tools to do so: he'll need to learn to read music and actually play or sing in front of others. History suggests that many children with autism really do have what it takes to be a musical performer, so be sure you don't sell your child short when you think about musical options.

DANCE THERAPY

According to the American Dance Therapy Association, "Dance/ Movement Therapy is the psychotherapeutic use of movement to promote emotional, cognitive, physical, and social integration of individuals." While dance therapy is relatively new and the research is scarce, there's good reason to believe that dance and movement can be wonderfully therapeutic for a child with autism. After all, kids with autism tend to have problems with body awareness, yet many crave movement and need the kind of sensory input that comes with activities like dance. At the same time, dance is more than just exercise: it's an art form. And like any art form, it can lead to a whole lifetime of enjoyment—as a participant, an observer, or both.

Dance therapy, however, is not dance. In many ways, its usefulness for the child with autism is similar to that of sensory-integration therapy. The differences are somewhat subtle: both are focused on providing sensory stimulation and teaching children the skills of sensory regulation. Dance, however, is less structured in terms of concrete goals and outcomes—but more focused on movement as communication and art. On a side note, it may be much harder to find a dance therapist than it is to find a sensory-integration therapist.

DRAMA THERAPY

Take a kid who has a hard time finding words, and give him a script. Then practice verbal interactions, emotional expression and recognition, humor, conversation, and social cuing in the nonjudgmental context of a therapeutic activity. That's what drama therapy is all about. Unlike music and dance therapy, drama therapy is really only useful for children who are both verbal and able to read; like music and dance therapy, though, drama therapy places therapeutic activity in the context of an art form that can become an area of lifelong interest.

Cindy Schneider is a pioneer in the field of drama therapy for people with autism, and author of the book *Acting Antics: A Theatrical Approach to Teaching Social Understanding to Kids and Teens with Asperger Syndrome*. Her classes in theater and movement are offered to kids and adults of all ages and with a fairly wide range of diagnoses (high-functioning autism, Asperger syndrome, PDD-NOS, nonverbal learning disorder, ADHD, etc.). According to Cindy, participants may gain:

- self-confidence, not only in performing but in interactions
- improved self-esteem and pride in their accomplishments
- improved recognition of emotions in others
- improved identification and labeling of own emotions
- new leisure-time activity in a group where they can be successful
- new awareness of volume levels and beginning modulation of level
- new skills for functioning as part of a group
- new skills for following directions
- improved ability to interact with peers
- increased self-confidence through success.

While music therapy is quite different from actually learning to read music and perform, drama therapy is surprising similar to putting on a show. If you're lucky enough to have a drama therapist nearby, your child's experience in drama therapy may be a terrific lead-in to taking part in an actual community theater—with or without you by her side.

And by the way, community theaters are always hungry for new talent, both behind and in front of the scenes. That means you, your spouse, and your other children may find yourselves painting sets, learning lines, or otherwise participating in community theater as a result of your autistic child's budding theatrical interests. Things could be worse!

Special-needs-only performing arts program

If your child is interested in the performing arts but is clearly not ready to be involved in a typical production, it makes sense to consider a special-needs performing arts program. These are fairly unusual, but they are out there—and if there is no such thing in your area, you may feel it's worthwhile to create one.

Finding a special-needs-only performing arts program starts, most of the time, with word of mouth research and a Google search. For example, a quick Google search of "Boston, Autism, Dance" sent me directly to the Boston Conservatory where I found the Boston Conservatory Program for Students on the Autism Spectrum. According to the website, "This first-of-its-kind conservatory program pairs students on the autism spectrum with Boston Conservatory music education graduate students for weekly lessons. Students, ages 9–17, also receive support from a 'consult team' that includes a music therapist, a speech pathologist, special educators, as well as professional musicians and music educators with a diagnosis on the autism spectrum." Even if a program just like this one doesn't exist in your region, a similar program—in music, dance, or drama—is likely to be available.

If you live in a more rural area or the offerings in your metropolitan area are meager, you may want to take a peek at a video called *Autism: The Musical* and "The Miracle Project" website. Elaine Hall is a California autism mom who took it upon herself to put on a full-scale, original musical, starring children with autism and their siblings. The results were both an outstanding production and the creation of a nonprofit dedicated to helping other families to follow in Elaine's footsteps. One of the most heartening outcomes of the original *Autism: The Musical* presentation, to my mind, is the fact that several children in the show went on to do much more with their musical talent. Since the kids in the show were, for the most part, relatively low-functioning, this achievement is especially impressive. See Appendix 3 of this book for more about "The Miracle Project" and autism-only or special-needs performing arts programs.

Semi- and full inclusion in the performing arts
Drama
When Tom was small (ages 4–8), he seemed to learn most of his spoken language by memorizing scripts from television shows and videos. This phenomenon, called "echolalia," is fairly common among kids with autism. And, like many kids with autism, while Tom wasn't actually inventing his own novel sentences and phrases, he was using his memorized lines appropriately. Yes, he sometimes sounded

uncannily like Thomas the Tank Engine or Theodore Tugboat—but on the other hand, he was communicating.

It seemed to me that, if Tom could memorize lines and recite them so well on his own, a drama class might be just the ticket. We didn't know anything about drama therapy at that point, but we did know that a local arts center offered drama classes to young children. So, we enrolled our son.

The truth is that Tom wasn't quite ready for full inclusion. So, I shadowed him on stage for about the first six months. The drama teacher was an absolutely terrific young woman just out of college, who had a lot of wonderful ideas for getting young children engaged in expressing themselves through theater. Interestingly to me, though she had no therapeutic background at all,

Phil (age 17) as King Reginald and Lena (age 12) as Queen Minerva in the teen musical "Princess and the Pea" in August 2009 at Acting Antics in Downingtown, PA

many of her exercises seemed designed precisely for the needs of a child with autism. Among her drama exercises:

- Show an emotion when it's called out (show me *angry!*).
- Try to make another person laugh.
- Become part of a moving machine made up of lots of kids.
- Tell a story that other kids act out.
- Act out a story that other kids tell.

None of these exercises is special, unusual, or therapeutic by design: they're simply part of the repertoire of a drama teacher. As Tom's mom, my job was to be sure he really heard and understood the directions and was ready to take his turn. And, by golly, he did a wonderful job of showing emotions, acting silly, and even telling a rambling story that could be acted out by other kids in the group.

As he got older, Tom's skills fell behind—and his interest waned. But by then he had already shown an interest in music, and we were heading in a whole new direction. Other youngsters with special needs, however, have found a real home in theater.

Because Tom has a "high-functioning autistic" or PDD diagnosis, his language skills are somewhat compromised. But children with Asperger syndrome are far better equipped to be dramatic, learn lines, and truly be a part of a theatrical production. In fact, kids with Asperger syndrome often find that memorizing lines and becoming someone else allows them to fit in in a whole new way. What's more, kids who are truly into theater are a breed apart. They're not athletic; they may be deliberately eccentric; they dress, move, and interact differently. For some kids with Asperger syndrome, community theater—or the school drama club—can be heaven on earth.

A NOTE TO PARENTS ABOUT AUTISTIC INCLUSION IN THEATER

As a parent, you may need to keep a close eye on your autistic child's involvement in community or school plays. Directors typically have very little patience for an actor with poor self-discipline or self-management skills—and your child's unintended disruptions can lead to bad feelings. What's more, community theater can be quite demanding. Kids may be asked to learn choreography for a musical comedy or have complex stage directions to memorize. Kids with autism—even kids with Asperger syndrome—may find the need to take notes, memorize extensive movements, or even manage choreography to be overwhelming. You may need to be present to take notes on your child's behalf or to step in if the lights, sound, crowds, or expectations seem to be leading toward a meltdown.

Music

Autism and music go together like bread and butter. Some of the world's greatest composers (Mozart and Beethoven, to name two) are suspected to have been autistic. Many people with autism, whether verbal or nonverbal, high- or low-functioning, have tremendous musical talent. Some people with autism have perfect pitch (the ability to sing and/or name a note with no reference point). Others are musically intuitive to an amazing

Tom Cook playing piano on the stage of the Kimmel Center in Philadelphia (a never-to-be-repeated opportunity!)

degree. And even if your child just enjoys plinking around on the piano, there may be real benefits to learning how to play a musical instrument or sing.

Music instruction is not the same thing as music therapy, as I mentioned earlier. Instruction is not intended to provide therapeutic results: it's intended to help your child play or sing. The outcome of learning to play an instrument or sing, however, can be tremendously therapeutic. A few possible outcomes are that:

- your child learns a skill that can be applied in a wide range of social settings
- your child builds a sense of self-confidence and personal pride
- your child learns to present himself on stage and to accept compliments graciously
- your child learns to take constructive criticism
- your child learns to perform as part of an ensemble
- your child builds fine-motor and listening skills
- your child develops a skill that will make him a welcome part of a community for the rest of his life
- your child discovers a passion that can lead to a career.

It's not always easy to find an instructor who's willing to teach a child with autism. It's almost certainly easiest when your child is young, assuming she's verbal and relatively high functioning. The Suzuki method (based on listening and imitation) may be a good choice for a young child with autism. If your child is not verbal, high functioning, or very young, though, finding a good instructor will take work.

I did quite a bit of calling around before I found a young, creative instructor willing to take on our son as a music student. Even the word *autism* turned off quite a few potential teachers—and if the word was too much to handle, I assumed my son would be too much as well. But Desiree wasn't scared: she'd already begun teaching one boy on the spectrum and figured she'd be able to handle another. She was right.

Of course, for the first few weeks, our then seven-year-old spent a good part of his clarinet lesson stuffing the bell of the clarinet with pocket toys. It was then that his instructor decided it would be a good idea to work on piano and clarinet at the same time—and what a great call that was!

Within a year, Tom was playing both piano and clarinet—and performing at recitals. During his first year, he was the only performer to play two instruments and among the few performers with really no stage fright at all! By the time he was in fourth grade, he was well ahead of his peers when we enrolled him in the school band. By the time he was in fifth grade, he was playing in the jazz ensemble, taking part in a typical band-camp program with no special support, and studying under a professor at a major music school in Boston.

Don't get me wrong: Tom is no prodigy, and while he's a solid clarinetist, he's not banging down the conservatory doors. What he is doing, though, is taking part in a group activity as a valued part of the ensemble. And that, for us, is what it's all about.

Stephen Shore is an adult with autism who has earned his Masters degree in Music Education. He plays trumpet, trombone, French horn, baritone horn, tuba, piano, flute, recorder, and a smattering of other things. He's also one of the very few people in the world who specifically teaches music skills to kids with autism. Here's Stephen's take on how to teach music and the autistic learner:

> Having autism can be an asset for a musician: it can lead to greater sensitivity to music. You just need to zero in on the right learning style. Music is a great entry for social interaction: music is a form of communication. In autism, the music centers are intact—plus, music is fun!
>
> I started with piano and learned how not to teach! The standard approach just doesn't work—it's too much talking. But I liked music, and I just kept going. I discovered the band, which meant I had a structured activity based on a deep interest. During high school, I spent lots of time in the band room, trying out different instruments.
>
> Usually I start with piano or recorder. If you throw the recorder, it won't break; you learn one note at a time, working on breath control and motor control. The piano is a very visual instrument: all the keys are there to be seen. So unless there's a burning desire for another instrument, I start on those. It

can be tough to get started, but once autistic kids catch up, it's amazing.

To find a teacher, I recommend posting signs at schools of music, education, and psychology. Find someone who's attracted to the challenge; then see how they interact with your child. They should be able to determine your child's learning style, whether it's visual, aural, or kinesthetic.

If your child is interested in school band, support should be provided. There are sensory issues to consider, and choice of instrument may be based on where you play. Flutes and sax sit in front; percussion is in the back. You can talk with the band leader or teacher to strategize. You'll also need to be sure the bandleader provides direct instruction to teach terminology, which can be tough for a child with autism.

There's nothing out there right now, so try, experiment, see what works.

Dance

The reality is that dance is an undiscovered country for most people with autism. There's no really good reason for this; in fact, many people with autism love movement and have a good memory for choreography. If your child with autism seems to enjoy movement, there's no reason to avoid signing her up for a dance class.

It's important, though, to let the dance instructor know of your child's special needs and challenges—and in particular, it's important to describe any issues your child may have with language processing and focus. Dance has its own language; and while, for example, your daughter may be a very capable ballerina, she may have real challenges in understanding or following the terms her teacher may toss out as she instructs the group.

Top tips for autism and the arts

- Don't assume your child can't sing, play, dance, draw, or paint, even if her verbal skills are compromised or nonexistent.

- Carefully consider whether therapy, a special-needs program, or inclusion is right for your child. Even if you decide to start slow, it's worth your while to experiment with inclusion. You may be surprised at what your child can really do!

- Consider the possibility that your child's interest in the arts could be a jumping-off place for the whole family. If your child loves to dance or act, you could wind up creating costumes, while your typical child gets involved with sets. If your child has a real musical talent, you may wind up being band parents.

- Be patient. Your child with autism may take a long time to learn the basics, but once he does, he may quickly surpass the skills of other children his age.

- Support passions. The arts have the potential to be areas of lifelong interest—and can even lead to social or professional achievements. And while your child's passions may seem "over the top" in typical settings, they may be absolutely average in artistic circles.

- Have fun! The arts are all about enjoyment and self-discovery. With and through your child, you have an opportunity to discover a whole new world of self-actualization.

Tip sheet

On the next pages is a tip sheet that you should copy and share with professionals, teachers, and therapists in the arts who will be working with your child or other children on the autism spectrum.

Tip sheet for welcoming kids and teens with autism to your arts program

Congratulations! You have a new member of your arts program who is going to gain tremendously from his or her involvement in your community. As someone who will be interacting with this young person and his or her family, your enthusiastic and creative support will make all the difference—not only to the young person but also to the family and even to your whole class or group.

As you develop your plans for inclusion, it's a good idea to tap into any resources you may have in the arts-therapy community. Even though you're not providing art therapy, many of the lessons learned through arts therapy may be helpful to you as you develop ways to make inclusion work effectively. In addition, these tips may help you get started:

1. Know that every autistic child is unique. If you've met or worked with an autistic child in the past, it's very possible that your new group member will surprise you.

2. Find out about your new group member and his family. Ask his parents for any useful information they can provide about his special challenges and abilities. Be sure to ask about his past experiences with and knowledge of your area of the arts: kids with autism may have fewer experiences with the arts than their typical peers, but they may also have special talents and abilities.

3. If your new group member can tell you about herself, be sure to ask her whether she has any specific concerns or anxieties.

4. Start with the basics. Instead of assuming that the child with autism already knows the rules and expectations associated with your area of the arts, assume that she doesn't. The truth is that other children in the group may also be able to use a refresher in the basics.

5. Use visual and hands-on teaching tools. You may be used to telling kids what they need to know, but kids with autism may have a tough time with verbal instructions. You can demonstrate, write down your instructions, or even offer hand-over-hand

help so that your group member with autism really "gets" your message.

6. Give direct instructions. Some children can accurately guess what's coming next or where you're headed when you begin to provide direction. Kids with autism can't. You'll need to be very direct in telling your group member with autism where to go, what to do, and when to do it. You may need to provide reminders to help him stay focused.

7. Be aware of possible sensory issues. Kids with autism may have unusual concerns about smells, loud noise, or physical sensations. Of course, you can't change your entire curriculum, but sticky paste can be replaced with a glue stick, music can be turned down, and the group as a whole can be asked to keep the noise level down to a dull roar.

8. Use other group members as peer buddies. Most groups include at least a few kids who are good at and enjoy helping others. If you can, team your autistic group member up with a buddy who's willing to lend a helping hand. During breaks, the buddy or buddies can spend a little extra time practicing or just hanging out with your autistic group member.

9. Use your new group member's parents as aides. It's quite possible that your autistic group member will need extra help in adjusting to your routine or handling the expectations of your program. If you have the time and inclination, you can certainly work with him. But it's absolutely fine to ask his mom or dad to help out when necessary or to let his parents know what skills to work on.

10. Don't lower your expectations. It's tempting to allow a child with autism to do his own thing, especially if he's quiet while he does so. But unless you run into serious behavior issues (which you should address with the child's parents), it's important to find a way to include your autistic group member in every aspect of your arts program.

Chapter 9

Summer Camps and the Natural World

Summer camps are not necessarily focused on the natural world, and vice versa. But the two often go together. Certainly, summer and nature exploration are a natural pairing. Typically, kids and their parents enjoy at least a portion of the summer together—whether at the beach, in the woods, at a lake, or just under a hose or sprinkler. Summer is, after all, about having fun in a less restrictive setting than school.

Except, all too often, for kids with autism and their families.

Working on the assumption that kids with autism can't manage change of any sort, families often struggle to find, fund, or create highly structured summer programs for their children with autism. When both parents work, this can be very challenging and expensive. Even when one parent is at home, the idea of creating and providing sufficient structure for a child with autism—all day, every day—along with therapies and social-skills coaching can be very daunting.

What are the real options for kids with autism during the summer? Of course, as with everything autism-related, the answer is "it depends." In rare cases, it really is necessary to provide a highly structured, therapeutic, self-contained program (more on this later).

But even for children who may have limited verbal or social abilities, the options are far broader than you might imagine.

Extended School Year: An American institution

Extended School Year (ESY) is an American program that may provide a disabled child with services during the summer months. ESY programming should be offered to a student who regresses significantly in academic, social, and/or related skills that are outlined in that child's Individualized Education Program (IEP) when the child is out of school for an extended period of time.

ESY, like most other special-education programs, varies from state to state and even from school to school. Some schools test for regression during winter break, while others test for regression throughout the school year. Some schools offer virtually all autistic children some form of ESY; others are willing to go to court over the question of whether ESY is appropriate.

It's important to note that ESY programs are developed differently by each school district. As a result, they vary dramatically in scope, style, and quality. In general, however, ESY programs are school-based, involve relatively little recreational activity, and last for only a few weeks.

Depending upon your child's needs and abilities (and on your school district), it may be possible to get ESY funding for inclusion in typical or specialized summer camps that cater specifically to children with autism-spectrum disorders (or that, alternatively, offer your child an opportunity for appropriate inclusion). Unfortunately, this is rarely the case—and as budgets shrink, such generous funding is becoming rarer and rarer.

If you live in the U.S., have limited resources and time, and simply need to have your child with autism in an ESY setting, you may say "yes" to the program just to know your child is in good hands. We certainly did do that, for two years in row. In both cases, ESY was only a part-time solution: the program ended at 1p.m. and ran for only about six weeks (typically, the American summer holiday runs from about mid- to late June to late August or early September).

It was true that Tom was in good hands (by sheer good luck, he was with his excellent kindergarten teacher). And he probably got something positive from the experience. But there were two issues that disturbed us.

First, the program was really intended as a summer-school experience: kids stayed inside for most of the day and worked on academics, handwriting, and similar skills. Of course, these skills are important; but we had hoped that summer would bring greater emphasis on activities like game playing, playground skills, and other outdoor, social pursuits.

Second, the program offered our son none of the fun or new experiences we associate with summer. There was no water play, no woods walks, no messy arts and crafts, no field trips. Much as we understood our son's limitations, we also knew that he needed to see, do, and experience more than was available in a structured classroom-based program.

The problem was that we seemed to have few options. As a toddler, Tom had had access to a "wrap-around" aide who could shadow him at a tiny day camp. But once he was in school, we had school programs or nothing. And "nothing" didn't seem to us to be a viable option, especially since we were both working close to full time.

It was time to look into summer camps.

Summer camps and autism

As with sports leagues and youth groups, summer-camp options for kids with autism are divided into the specialized, the semi-inclusive, and the inclusive. Unlike sports leagues and youth groups, though, camps are also divided into the outrageously expensive, the moderately expensive, and the relatively inexpensive. Naturally, camps (especially sleep-away camps) that are intended specifically for children with special needs are at the very high end when it comes to cost (they can be very expensive for any child, irrespective of disability). Surprisingly, though, semi- and wholly-inclusive programs that accept kids with autism are not necessarily pricey at all. In some cases, families may also be able to find scholarships to underwrite their child's camp experience.

Specialized autism and special-needs-only summer camps

Specialized summer camps for children with autism range from local day camps to faraway sleep-away camps—and there are more and more such camps available as more parents are seeking specialized programs for their children with autism. Kids come from all over the world to attend these camps, which can be widely scattered (most seem to be in the United States, Canada, and Britain). Typically, autism-only camps are a nice mixture of ordinary summer-camp activities (swimming, games, arts and crafts, boating, nature walks, and so forth) and therapeutic programs focused on fostering social and communication skills. To provide a truly therapeutic, structured, autism-only experience, these camps have very low counselor-to-camper ratios—as low as one-to-two and rarely higher than one-to-three.

It is rare for a camp to accept children who are neither verbal nor potty trained (though of the two, potty training is by far the more important skill). That's because so many of the activities offered require some degree of verbal instruction—and it's very challenging indeed to change a diaper on a canoe! That said, there certainly are camps that cater to the most profoundly disabled children; those camps generally accept children with a broader range of disabilities, including physical challenges such as cerebral palsy.

It is less rare for a camp to accept only children with special needs that are relatively mild—including Asperger syndrome. In fact, there are now a whole raft of camps designed for children whose diagnoses include Asperger syndrome, ADD, ADHD, Tourettes, OCD, etc. These kids are verbal, physically capable, and able to follow direction and take part in challenging activities such as orienteering and ropes courses. On the other hand, these same kids may have a very tough time fitting into the social structure of typical camps, where flexibility and ability to handle group dynamics, physical challenges, and discomfort (heat, bugs, and the like) are critical.

If you plan to send your child with autism to a private summer camp for kids with autism or similar special needs, it's likely you'll be paying a good deal for your child's summer experience. In 2010, the cost of an autism-only sleep-away camp runs well over $1,000 per week; day camp may range up to $500 per week. You can save money by going through camps offered through organizations such as the YMCA, JCC, Variety Clubs, or Easter Seals—and/or you can apply for grants or "camperships" that may support a portion of your child's experience.

The great advantage of a camp that caters specifically to your child's needs is, of course, that the camp caters specifically to your child's needs. Staff is trained to manage autism, and many staff members are professionals in the field of special education or autism therapy. This is important both for your child and for you, the parent. Your child can depend upon a schedule, program, food, and support that make it easy to take part in camp experiences. And you can depend upon a summer during which your child with autism will be accepted and made welcome. If, like us, you've had your child booted from a program for odd behaviors, lack of attention to directions, or inability to socialize, you'll know how wonderful it is to know your child's differences won't present a problem.

The disadvantages of a special-needs-only camp include the high cost and the fact that your child with autism is spending all of his or her time completely surrounded by peers with similar disabilities. This latter fact is significant, depending upon the child, because (1) it is very hard to learn social skills when your only peers are as socially challenged as you are, and (2) you are living in an artificially designed world in which supports and accommodations are laid out without question, sometimes even when they aren't strictly speaking necessary. This may mean that your child may be denied the opportunity to expand her own horizons, challenge her limits, or surprise herself. One of the best aspects of typical summer camp is that kids who, for whatever reason, did poorly in school can suddenly shine in a whole new setting.

One other disadvantage of a special-needs-only camp in this day and age is that the focus of the camp is, well, special needs. This means that the camp can't cater to your child's particular interests or passions. Typical kids (and autistic kids in typical camps) get to choose from an incredible array of specialized camp programs, ranging from computer programming to wilderness adventures. Special-needs kids in a special-needs camp have their activities preselected and carefully managed to ensure a positive experience for all. If your child really has no particular interest in a particular type of camp, that's fine; if she does, she may be missing out on an opportunity to meet and work with typical peers who actually share her passions.

Semi-inclusive camps

Because our son is neither very high functioning nor very disabled, we had a tough time finding just the right camp setting for him. Locally, we could find options for special-needs-only programs (which we felt were too restrictive) and typical camps (which would simply overwhelm our son). What to do?

In the long run, we worked with the local YMCA to start up a semi-inclusive day camp for kids on the autism spectrum (more on this later). In the meanwhile, though, I did a great deal of research to find out what was available. And what I found were a number of very different types of semi-inclusive models:

- Some camps offered aides who would support kids with special needs as they took part in a variety of typical programs.

- Some camps had autism-only "bunks" (groups) incorporated into a typical camp.

- Some offered reverse inclusion: typically developing kids either attended the camp or came in to act as role models and mentors at certain times of the day or week.

- Some accepted both autistic children and their typically developing siblings—an interesting and, for some, very handy alternative.

All these approaches seemed to me to offer the best of all worlds: autism-oriented supports and an understanding of autistic differences, combined with interaction with typical peers and the possibility of taking part in more challenging activities or experiences. The costs of semi-inclusive camps are lower than the costs of autism-only camps. And even better for many parents, semi-inclusive camps are open to typically developing peers.

The down-side of semi-inclusion, though, is that the staff tends to be made up largely of well-intentioned but poorly trained teens and young adults who have relatively little experience working with kids on the autism spectrum. Programs are not set up with autism in mind, which means that kids with autism may be confronted with difficult situations such as abrupt changes in schedule, muddy playing fields, too much noise and heat, etc. While some kids with autism do much better than parents anticipate in such circumstances, some don't.

Typical day camps

When I first broached the subject of summer camp to a group of parents of children with Asperger syndrome, I learned that most of their kids were actually attending typical day camp with no support. This amazed me, until I learned that most of their kids were actually attending the *same* camp, one that was very small, very structured, and well-known to all the parents in the group.

While my son couldn't have attended a typical day camp without one-on-one support when he was very young, by the time he was ten, he could. Like the parents in the support group, I found a very small, very structured camp where there were plenty of counselors (mostly teenagers, sometimes called CITs or "counselors in training") and relatively low-key expectations for the campers. My son was one of the oldest kids there, and he attended with his sister (a big plus).

We had no expectations that the camp program would be therapeutic in any way, but we did hope our kids would have fun, have a few new experiences, and make it through the week with no "issues." Our hopes, it turned out, were not high enough. While Tom didn't make any fast friends, he got along with the other kids with no problem. He took part in every activity without meltdowns (with the

Teen-aged Cubby Elder in a tree with his climbing harness, at home in Chicopee, MA

exception of feeding the sheep—it turns out the sound of sheep bleating drives him crazy!). And he did, for the first time, connect on a personal level with a number of animals including ponies, rabbits, puppies, and goats. In short, the experience was terrific!

Obviously not all kids with autism can attend a typical day camp without support. And not every kid with Asperger syndrome or high-functioning autism can attend camp without an aide. But clearly, the smaller and more structured the setting, the more likely it is to work out. That said, here are a few tips for selecting and managing a typical day camp experience.

KNOW WHAT YOU'RE GETTING INTO

If possible, visit the camp with your child during the summer before you intend to enroll. Be absolutely certain the camp administration understands and is comfortable with your child's challenges and has a specific plan for managing any predictable issues or concerns.

PROVIDE AS MUCH INFORMATION AS YOU CAN

Some camps will actively ask you to provide your child's IEP (if you have one); others might ask you for advice on how to support your child. If the camp doesn't ask, provide the information anyway. If possible, meet with your child's counselors ahead of time to provide ideas, answer questions, and open the doors of communication.

CHOOSE WISELY

Your neighbor's kid may love the camp down the road, but that doesn't mean it's right for your child with autism. Look around carefully before making a selection.

KEEP IT SMALL

Big camps may offer a wide range of activities, but they can easily become overwhelming and difficult to manage. The social interactions among kids may also be more complex when there are more possible cliques and conflicts.

CONSIDER SENDING YOUR OWN ONE-ON-ONE AIDE

If your school or another agency (or the camp) offers a one-on-one aide, it's probably a good idea to say "yes"—unless your child objects strenuously. If the aide turns out to be unnecessary, you'll know for next year. Of course, hiring your own one-on-one aide is another (pricey) option.

STAY ON TOP OF THE SITUATION

Be sure to check in with the staff each day to know what kinds of issues are arising and how they're being handled. Don't allow staff to shunt you off with a statement like, "He did great." Depending upon the staffer, that could mean anything from, "He made a friend for the first time" to "He didn't actually whack anyone with a stick."

OFFER TO PROVIDE HELP, IDEAS, AND SUPPORT

If camp counselors (often teens and young adults with little training) are unsure how to help your child to get involved, make friends, or understand rules, help them out. Provide them with whatever you think might help. In our case, it was helpful to let counselors know that our son's "pocket toys" were (and are) key to his security—and as such, they were not to be shared.

HAVE A BACK-UP PLAN

Even the best-laid plans can go awry, and if your child winds up being asked to leave, you'll need to have an alternate "Plan B" for your child's summer.

Typical sleep-away camps

Quite honestly, it's unlikely that you'll find that a typical sleep-away camp is a good match for a child with autism. Between the bugs, the heat, the sleeping and eating conditions, the camper-to-counselor ratios (typically one adult and one teen to about twelve kids) the social demands, and the many brand-new experiences, there are just too many ways to run into problems. There may, however, be a few exceptions, based upon your particular circumstances. Here are a few possibilities to consider:

- Some YMCA sleep-away camps actually provide support to children with autism. This is rare, but it's certainly worth your while to ask your local YMCA about such programs.

- Boy and Girl Scout troops often take part in overnight camping and summer-camp experiences. If your child with autism is a part of a troop, he or she may be ready to join the troop at camp. As is described in Chapter 5, Scouts and other organizations are now much more open to allowing parents to come along—a nice option if your child is autistic.

- Special-interest camps (circus camp, computer camp, karate camp, etc.) may be options for a very high-functioning child who is passionate about a particular activity. In fact, such a camp has the potential to be a terrific opportunity for bonding with kids and adults who truly share an intense interest. The trick, of course, is to be sure that the camp is also physically comfortable for your autistic child, who may have issues with lumpy mattresses, questionable food, etc.

- Family camps are now becoming more and more popular, and you may wish to try out the camp experience with your child at such a camp. Since the actual activities are similar to those your child would experience at a youth-only camp (boating, swimming, hiking, sleeping in cabins, eating in a mess hall, etc.), you and your child will be able to see for yourselves whether the experience is right for him. (More on family camps later in this chapter.)

- Your child with autism may be able to attend a typical sleep-away camp with a sibling or close friend who acts as a peer buddy. The up-side of this is that your child with autism may have a positive experience; the down-side is that her "peer buddy" is likely to have a much tougher time enjoying camp and just being a kid.

- You can become your child's support staff by becoming a counselor or employee at a summer camp. Of course, you can't go with your child to every activity if you're working, but you can be available to troubleshoot or manage difficult situations if and when they arise.

- You can hire or get access to an aide who is able to shadow your child at camp. This is a tricky project since finding such a person, paying her, and then arranging for their presence at camp are all tough to arrange.

If you do decide to send your child with autism to a typical sleep-away camp, it's very important to communicate your child's needs to the camp administration. It's equally important to chat with and communicate with his bunk counselors. Bear in mind that you do have the option of, for example, providing special food for your child, sending along your child's own blankets, and otherwise ensuring that your child is physically comfortable. After all, you're shelling out good money for the experience! If the administration tells you that special needs are not accommodated at the camp, it's probably the wrong camp for your autistic child.

Finding a camp for your child with autism

It's easy enough to search directories for "autism camps," and you'll find plenty of listings on sites such as MySummerCamps.com (more directories and websites are listed in Appendix 3). The question of whether any individual camp is right for your child is a whole different issue, and it may take some digging, experimenting, and flexibility to find the right match.

As is often the case, a good way to start your search is to begin with your own personal parameters and concerns. For example:

- What's your budget? If you have $500, a $10,000 camp—no matter how terrific—is unlikely to be a good match.

- Do you feel your child would do best in a special-needs, semi-inclusive, or inclusive setting?

- Are you seeking a therapeutic program or just a fun summer experience?

- How far will you travel? If you're working full-time and sending your child to day camp, your options are obviously limited. You may also prefer a program that's nearby, simply because you can continue to connect with the same families and kids over the course of the year.

- Must this camp accept both your autistic child and her typical siblings? If so, you're looking for a semi-inclusive, inclusive, or typical camp that's able to provide positive experiences for a wide range of children.

- Are you looking for specific activities? Some well-staffed, highly regarded summer-camp programs are offered at schools that are empty for the summer. They may offer a wide range of activities, but swimming and boating are unlikely to be among them.

Once you have a gist of what you're looking for, ask around. Talk with parents in your child's school, in your local autism-support group, and online. In this situation, it's best to find and connect with families whose children are similar to yours in terms of age, abilities, interests, and challenges. Even so, of course, one child's fabulous summer is another child's disaster; but by asking plenty of questions, you should be able to get a sense as to whether a particular camp really might be a good choice for your child.

As I recommended for typical camp programs, you'll want to visit the camp at least once and preferably more than once. You'll also want to get names of parents whose children have attended the camp and call them. Be sure you ask them really relevant questions: Johnny may have had a terrific time with the horseback riding, but how did the counselors handle kids' frustrations, personality conflicts, or meltdowns? Is there a disciplinary system in place? How well does the camp communicate with parents? While it's helpful to talk with the camp director about these issues, it's even more helpful to get a parents'-eye view.

Creating a camp for your child with autism

They say necessity is the mother of invention. As the parent of a son with PDD-NOS (in my son's case, high-functioning autism), I tend to agree. Camp Outlook, a semi-inclusive day camp for children on the spectrum, was invented for our son Tom when he was six years old—and, as it turned out, for autistic children throughout the Philadelphia area.

Dov Shestack on a camping trip in Southern California, 2001

Of course, creating a day camp isn't for everyone. But as you'll see, the process was relatively straightforward, and because we were working with a nonprofit with an inclusive mission that had vast experience with running camp programs, I was able to step away from the actual day-to-day work involved with running a day camp. The bottom line is that, if there are no local resources available, your best alternative may be to take matters into your own hands and take creative action.

Like so many families with autistic children, we had a paltry few summer options, none of them good. Typical camp was not an option, at least, not without a nonexistent one-on-one aide. Camps for disabled children were non-inclusive and largely geared to children with physical differences. Our district did offer ESY, but it turned out to be a partial-day summer school heavy on the academics and light on the social skills.

So, armed with my autism statistics, research on local camp programs, a proposed camp program, and even a proposed budget, I called on our local YMCA. As a fundraising consultant, I'd worked for YMCAs across the country for years, and I knew these people would help if they could.

At our first meeting, I described the autism spectrum and its characteristics. And I assured them that—though they didn't know it—they'd been serving autistic kids for years. Those kids who zoned out during arts and crafts or didn't quite seem to grasp the concept of competitive sports were almost certainly on the spectrum. I explained that most autistic kids could join in a camp experience with support and encouragement. Even children with limited verbal skills could get a great deal out of a supportive, inclusive summer program.

Indeed, the Ambler area YMCA, part of the Philadelphia metropolitan YMCA, was willing to consider the idea of an inclusive program for autistic youth. We talked further, and it turned out that their swim coach just happened to have considerable autism experience and background and would be available to help set up the program.

By March, we had a grant for $10,000 from a local foundation. Staff was hired. And—most surprising to the YMCA, who expected to lose money on the camp—three school districts had selected Camp Outlook as their ESY setting and were underwriting the costs and supplying transportation for their students. The camp manager was reviewing IEPs hand-over-fist to ensure that the Y would be able to support camp registrants appropriately.

By June, Camp Outlook was completely booked, with 12 children per week for eight weeks for a total of 25 children served. Y staff ran an initial parent meeting, and the program was launched.

In the first year, the program was simple. Camp Outlook campers had their own "homeroom," which was set up with quiet spaces (tents) and sensory activities. A lead counselor with special-needs experience worked with three other counselors to provide a one-to-three ratio. Camp Outlook campers were included with typical age peers during the mornings (with one-to-three support), taking part in arts and crafts, sports, drama, and more. They swam separately in the afternoon with one-to-two support and had their own cooking and science activities. Most impressive, every single Camp Outlook camper successfully took part in whole-camp field trips to places as challenging as Crystal Cave and a small water park. Overall, the program was a successful pilot, but I could see opportunities to improve (and, of course, expand!).

During the second year, additional YMCAs in the area announced plans to create their own Camp Outlook programs based on the Ambler model, and two other area Ys indicated their plans to do the same in the following year. Through another parent, a neighboring association of YMCAs has become interested in Camp Outlook programs of their own. We even began conversations with the faculty at Temple University's Therapeutic Recreation Department to allow therapeutic recreation students to earn credit through their work with Camp Outlook campers.

Clearly, the concept of a semi-inclusive camp for kids on the autism spectrum has legs—not only for families like ours but for the Y as well. By running a camp program for ASD children, the YMCA fulfills its mission, wins grants, and earns kudos. By supporting the program—and the Y—we're making it work for our kids.

Family camps

The concept of a family camp is not new; families have been going to camps of one sort or another for well over 100 years. But in the last 15 years (at least, according to the *Boston Globe*), the number of family camps has increased by 215 percent. The *Globe* suggests this may be the result of the economic recession, but I suspect it may also have to do with the rise of special-needs diagnoses.

As more and more kids are diagnosed—rightly or wrongly— with autism-spectrum disorders, ADHD, Tourettes, and a myriad of other disorders, it becomes tougher and tougher to find an ordinary camp that will just say "yes" to including your child. Family camps allow parents to say "yes" to their kids, to summer, to fun, and to adventure—without anyone else's permission or support.

Family camps range from the very basic (a cabin, a waterfront, a mess hall) to the very elaborate (four-poster beds at a high-class country inn). They can include all kinds of sports and activities that make it possible for whole families to enjoy what they like, split up as necessary, and still enjoy a campfire and evening sing-along together.

While your child with autism may not be ready for waterskiing or stilt walking, she may be ready to take a nature hike, try fishing, or just paddle around in a lake. And while she may not connect on a personal level with many other kids at the camp, it's easy to find opportunities to socialize on a very low-key level. Maybe your child could hand out marshmallows at a campfire, show off the fish she caught at dinner time, join in a sing-along, or take the lead during a nature hike. If things do get out of hand for any reason and your child has behavioral issues, you have your own cabin available as a quiet spot. Of course, it helps to bring along personal comfort items such as blankets, toys, and even videos.

Where and how do you find family camps? Not to sound like a broken record, but the YMCA has a terrific reputation as a provider of family camps in the U.S., Canada, and the U.K. There's more information about family camp directories in Appendix 3 of this book.

Out into the natural world: Family camping

Camping isn't for everyone. It's wonderful when you find the right spot, the weather cooperates, there's plenty of firewood, and the neighbors are quiet. When any of those elements is not quite right, though, the outcome can be disastrous. That, of course, goes double for kids with autism, whose sensory issues or need for familiarity can make camping very tough.

On the other hand, we were amazed when we took our first family camping trip to find that Tom, more than any of us, was absolutely at ease at the campground. There's something very comforting about carrying your home along with you, and whether you're tent camping or driving an RV, you're essentially bringing part of your home on vacation.

Another great plus for camping is the peace and quiet. Unlike hotels, camps, or even your own home, campsites are technology-free. There are no television, no video games…just the sounds of crickets and the babbling brook. And even when there is a bit more going on, the feeling of being away from it all can be just as pleasant for a child with autism as it is for his parents and siblings.

Perhaps the most important plus about camping for a family with an autistic child is the lack of other adults or kids who are likely to judge your child, question your parenting, set up roadblocks, require paperwork, or otherwise make your life less pleasant. Out in the woods, you're just a family—and your child with autism is just a kid. If he flaps his hands, the bears don't care. If he eats nothing but peanut butter, so be it. And if he has no interest whatever in being nice, polite, or friendly to the neighbors, it really doesn't make the least bit of difference.

This book is not a guide to camping, and I'm no camping expert; but I can offer a few words of advice when it comes to camping with a child on the autism spectrum.

CHOOSE YOUR LOCATION WITH CARE
Campsites differ radically, and you'll want to check with travel guides and camping friends to be sure you choose an area that's comfortable, uncrowded, and easy to navigate. You'll also want to be sure the basic amenities (toilets, showers, and recreation) are available and easy to find.

DON'T GO TOO FAR FROM HOME
Unless and until your child with autism has become a veteran camper, give yourself an out. If things don't work out for any reason—sensory issues, anxiety, weather, mosquitoes—it's best to be able to head home quickly.

HAVE A PLAN
Even though relaxation is the point, you should be able to provide your child with at least some semblance of a schedule. In fact, if you can, it's best to provide your child with a visual plan of action.

BRING THE TOOLS YOU NEED TO EXPLORE AND HAVE FUN
A pair of field glasses (binoculars) is handy for both spotting wildlife and for viewing the stars. A net and bucket can turn a stroll along the beach into an afternoon of critter collecting.

GIVE YOUR CHILD A CHANCE TO EXPLORE—AND TAKE THE OPPORTUNITY TO ENJOY HIS COMPANY

We've noticed that our son sees the natural world in a different way from other kids: he's more observant of details, more willing to stand still and watch wildlife, and less likely to get bored during a woods walk. It's wonderful to see your autistic child's strengths, and to let him lead for once.

Day trips into the wild blue yonder (and spots closer to home)

If you or your kids feel that sleeping in the wild is a bit over the top, you can certainly get out into the wild for a few hours. Summer hikes, trips to the lake or beach, afternoons on the water, and other summer experiences can be wonderful opportunities for your child with autism to explore the world. At the same time, because they're such low-key, low-pressure adventures, they're usually easy on the whole family. Our son (and daughter) are crazy about the beach, and so are

Tom Cook discovers a live horseshoe crab at the beach in Falmouth, MA (2005)

we. As a result, we now live just minutes from the bay and even closer to a harbor. For our daughter, it's all very nice—but for our son, it's a wonderful place to grow up. It's Tom who discovered the American eels under the harbor; it's Tom who notices the herons standing silently in the tidal marsh; it's Tom who identifies the different bird songs; and it's Tom who can sit silently watching the swans paddle around a pond.

Of course, you can enjoy the natural world with an open-ended woods walk. For a child with autism, though, it may be necessary to have a little more structure in mind. You might also want to select experiences that have the potential to satisfy your child's interests or sensory needs—and avoid those that could be a little too adventurous. As always, it's important to have an escape route if things go awry, so a hike up to the top of a major peak may not be the best option. If your child suddenly decides he's unhappy up there, getting down will be quite a chore. With those caveats in mind, here are a few ideas to consider.

THE BEACH

If you live anywhere near the ocean, consider spending at least a few hours on the beach, at least a few times each summer. For many kids with autism, the sensory input of waves and sand is enormously calming (just as it is for everyone else). And the beach is one of the few places where kids with autism look and act just about like everyone else. If you don't believe me, take a few minutes to look around the next time you're at the shore. Notice the dads burying their kids in sand? The moms splashing their kids? The teens racing the waves like maniacs, acting as if they can't handle a drop of the cold, salty water on their skin? Now watch your child. Enjoy.

Tom Cook swimming at the
Abington PA YMCA

LAKES, RIVERS, BROOKS, STREAMS

Any body of water is a natural attractor for kids (and adults). And for some reason, that seems to go double for people with autism. Kids with autism can often spend hours just hanging out near, in, and on the water.

SHORT, WELL-TENDED WOODSY TRAILS

If you do go for a day hike with your child on the autism spectrum, be sure you know where you're headed—and that the trail is accommodating. At all costs, avoid trails that are likely to be laden with poison ivy, thick with mosquitoes, or otherwise likely to cause sensory issues. While some kids with autism are natural hikers with plenty of stamina, it's also important to note that many are not. In fact, autism can often go along with physical issues that make strenuous hikes very difficult.

NATURE CENTERS AND STATE OR NATIONAL PARKS

These carefully tended natural areas are ideal for exploring with an autistic child. They're well marked and mapped and often include a variety of water features. They also offer the opportunity for you to stand back and let your child with autism teach you a thing or two.

We've found that Tom has opened our eyes to all kinds of things we'd never noticed, from the tiny, wooly caterpillars on the ground to the hole in a tree where birds have built a nest. We've also found that exploring the natural world with our son has given us a new appreciation for the art of quiet, patient observation.

Tom Cook and a partner measuring animal tracks at the Cape Cod National Seashore's Junior Ranger program

Top tips for enjoying summer camps and the natural world

- Remember that autism in no way lessens your child's ability to enjoy the natural world. In fact, you and your child may have a much less stressful, more relaxing time in the natural world than among the demanding expectations of "typical" families.

- Select a summer camp carefully, based not only on descriptions and advice but also on personal visits.

- Select the type of camp (special-needs, semi-inclusive, inclusive) that is truly appropriate for your child. If your child is interested in a particular type of activity, consider sending her to a specialty camp where she can meet others with similar interests.

- Communicate with camp personnel as often as possible, and be sure you and they are "really" communicating. Young counselors may feel awkward telling adults that their child is simply not participating, so you may want to observe your child in action.

- If you want to "test the waters," or provide extra support to your child, consider a family camp or camping experience, or take an active role in your child's summer setting.

- When going out into the natural world, prepare ahead of time with your child's interests and abilities in mind. Consider starting in a "safe" setting such as a nature center or local park—or if you're hiking, select a short, easy hike.

Chapter 10

Special Interests, Clubs, Family Outings, and Other Ideas

If you're interested in taking part in a family activity that's specifically created to serve the needs of families living with autism, you've picked the right decade. A recent article in the *Baltimore Sun* made an excellent point when it described "a growing awareness of the needs of autistic children and their families as well as a desire to make sure they don't have to miss out on the everyday activities that most families may take for granted." What the author didn't make much of in this story ("Outings tailored for autistic kids," October 18, 2009) is the fact that there is gold in them thar hills. That is, a family with an autistic child is often willing to pay a premium price for a positive experience designed to include and accommodate the needs of their autistic child.

The article describes movies, dining experiences, museums, and an indoor children's gym, all of which had found ways to make it easy and pleasant to serve families with a special-needs child. As I've mentioned, it really isn't all that hard or expensive: turn down the music, offer a quiet place to "escape," and provide some form of visual preview of the experience. And, of course, don't go into a state of shock when a child has a meltdown, walks around when he should be sitting, or makes a strange noise. Even your local amusement arcade really should be able to pull that off!

So what kinds of outings and activities are available for families with an autistic child? While I've touched on many in this book, I've really only scratched the surface. Our family, like most, does a thousand and one things during the course of a year that just "come up." From a Renaissance Fair to family vacation, we take part in dozens of nonschool experiences—and while Tom has a tougher time with some than with others, he takes part in just about all of them. And by the way, where Tom may have a more difficult time engaging in or managing the sensory input from, say, a holiday parade, Sara may have an equally difficult time finding the patience to enjoy a star party (star gazing on the lawn with a group of amateur astronomers and their telescopes). My point is that being autistic doesn't guarantee you'll have a hard time with any given activity, and being neurotypical doesn't always guarantee success!

Eating out "nicely"

If your child with autism cannot sit still at a table and eat with a fork and knife, he should not be going out to eat at a nice restaurant. This is probably an unpopular statement; but at this point in history, there are so many restaurants where it *is* acceptable to get up, walk around, eat with your hands, and otherwise behave as you wish that there's simply no reason to spend your hard-earned money (or others') on a meal that will be unpleasant for all involved.

That said, there are ways to make it easier to eat out nicely, beginning with your home-education curriculum and including options for selecting or bringing food. Eating out at a restaurant requires your child to manage a number of social and physical expectations, but those expectations are almost always the same. That is, if you've been to one restaurant, you've been to most. That means you should be able to practice restaurant manners and procedures at home, and you might even want to get a copy of the restaurant's menu to use as a prop.

If your child is nonverbal or painfully shy, you may need to speak for him—though it's certainly great if he can say his piece on his own after practice. But even if you place his order, he can practice and perfect the art of sitting in his seat, putting his napkin in his lap, entertaining himself with crayons or a book as necessary, placing an order, eating his food, placing his utensils on the plate, and waiting patiently until the meal is finished. You can involve other siblings in the practicing process, having different people act as waiters and even using slightly different words (What will you have? Are you ready to order? What will the young man have?), so that your child knows that he should listen for the idea (What do you want to eat?) rather than a set of specific words. And, by the way, none of this practice will go to waste on typical siblings or other children, many of whom could almost certainly use more practice in eating like a civilized person.

If your child has severe sensory issues, dietary limitations, or other food-related issues, you may need to pack along certain foods. Before you decide to do this, you should contact the restaurant ahead of time to be sure it won't be a problem. The last thing you want, as you start a formal dinner at a restaurant, is to hear from the waiter that bringing in outside food is not allowed. We've found, though, that most restaurants are amenable to a family's packing in a small portion of the meal if it means that the rest of the family will be ordering off the menu (and, of course, paying full price for their food).

With the right practice, supports, and situation, your child with autism should be able to sit comfortably through at least a good portion of the meal. Of course, like any child, yours may find herself impatient or anxious. She may need to get up once or twice. But if she literally can't sit still for more than a minute or two or can't stop herself from making loud, repetitive noises, a "nice restaurant" just may be a poor choice: fast food may be the better option.

On a positive note, we've found that our hard work in preparing our kids for restaurant meals has paid off. Recently, a waitress at a local restaurant where we eat from time to time said, "Oh, it's so nice to see you. You're the family with the polite kids!" Since so few families these days really bother to work on skills like proper restaurant etiquette, it's quite possible that your child with autism, too, will gain a reputation for being the "polite kid" in town.

Community events and holiday celebrations

Very often, community events and holiday celebrations involve a lot of noise and confusion. Parades, fireworks, festivals, fairs, and the like are intended to fill the senses to overflowing, and they do. For the child with autism, these types of events can be too much—though with a few precautions and a good deal of patience, they can also become positive experiences.

The key to enjoying any large, loud community event with your autistic child is to have an easy, no-hassle, no-pain escape plan in place. It's quite possible your child will have a terrific time watching the Christmas parade or meeting the animals at the county fair. But it's just as possible that he won't—and that his behavior will make it impossible to stay. If a meltdown does seem imminent (or actually occurs), you need to know how you're going to handle the situation with the least amount of anxiety and upset possible. If you have other children attending the event, you'll need to know who's going to take your autistic child home and who's going to stay with the other children. Alternatively, depending upon your child and your situation, you may be able simply to move into a quiet space, allow your child to calm himself, and rejoin the event when he's ready.

All that said, there are some simple techniques you can employ to increase the chance that your experience will be positive—for your child and for your whole family. There are also some approaches that, particularly for a higher-functioning child, may make the experience truly memorable (in a good way).

KNOW WHAT YOU'RE GOING TO DO, AND HAVE A PLAN
Share your plan with everyone (including your spouse or partner).

PROVIDE A CLEAR PREVIEW OF WHAT YOU'RE GOING TO DO AND HOW IT WILL HAPPEN
For example, when we attend the county fair we're very clear: "*First*, we will visit the animals; *next*, we will get a snack; *then*, we will go on the rides. We know you prefer the slower rides, and Mom will ride with you. Sara likes the faster rides, and she will go with Dad. Then we'll all get together again to listen to music." If you possibly can, follow the plan closely.

IF THERE WILL BE A SENSORY ASSAULT (IN THE FORM OF VERY LOUD MUSIC, FIREWORKS, ETC.), PLAN FOR IT

Of course, one option is simply to leave before the event occurs. Another is to stand at the outskirts of the event, allowing you to see and hear but keeping the sound and intensity at a lower level. If even that level of intensity is too much, you're in a good position to leave early without coping with traffic.

COME EQUIPPED

We have attended fireworks displays with a pair of sound-deadening earphones for our son. In that way, Tom can enjoy the beauty of the fireworks without being overwhelmed by the sound.

DON'T EXPECT TOO MUCH

Many children on the spectrum can do well for an hour or two—and that's it. Knowing this, you can plan accordingly. Truth be told, most families with infants and toddlers need to plan with short-attention spans, naps, and early bedtimes in mind, so you certainly won't be alone in leaving early or finding a quiet spot where your child can regroup.

CONSIDER INCLUDING YOUR CHILD IN THE EVENT ITSELF

If your child with autism has raised a vegetable that's being exhibited at the fair, helped build a float for the parade, or is marching with his Scout troop or other organization, he may find himself able to manage the event more easily. Of course, this isn't always the case— and only you know your own child's abilities and limitations.

Family and community traditions

The up-side of traditions and the child with autism

Some community and family events are extremely predictable and are even identical year after year. Halloween, Christmas, Passover, Thanksgiving, and so forth can be so repetitive as to be boring to the average person—but people with autism may find that predictability comforting.

As a parent, you can take advantage of that predictability by creating durable scripts and photo albums to prepare your child for annual events. You can go through pictures of the people who will be present and practice greetings ("Hi, Aunt Jane," kiss kiss). You can even rehearse literal scripts ("Trick or treat! Thanks for the candy!"). While your child may sound a bit robotic as she recites her lines, most people will recognize the polite intent and respond in kind.

Tom and Sara Cook ready for Trick or Treating on Halloween

We've found that Tom likes to anticipate certain events in idiosyncratic ways. For example, while most children think happily about the joy of eating Halloween candy, Tom looks forward to planning the trick-or-treating route, drawing a face on a pumpkin, and trying out his costume. The candy is nice, but a few Hershey bars are enough for him.

Once, he drank cherry cola at a Passover seder, and now he looks forward to it each year, using the same words and facial expressions to describe the fizz. We join in on his anticipatory excitement, even if we don't personally share it. In fact, each Passover, we make a point of bringing along the bottle of (Kosher) cherry cola to be sure it's there—although it's hardly a cherished tradition of the Hebrew people!

It's this type of attention to small details that can make childhood memories for any child. Think back to your childhood memories, and you'll probably find it's the little things that spring to mind—the special ornaments, favorite foods and smells. It seems, though, that memory and tradition are even more significant to children with autism. Perhaps the reason is that so many people with autism have extraordinary visual, aural and/or olfactory memories; or maybe it's the intense pleasure derived from repetition. Whatever the reasons, though, it's easy and fun for parents and relatives to make and keep traditions.

The down-side of traditions and the child with autism

With all the plusses of family and community traditions, though, there are a few potential down-sides. While these issues can come up with any child, they're most likely to be a problem with kids on the autism spectrum.

One issue that may arise is an unexpected change in plans. A snowstorm or illness can throw holiday plans into turmoil, something that's tough on everyone but hardest on the child with autism. Similarly, Grandma may have decided that this is the year to throw all her traditions aside and create a Hawaiian luau for Christmas dinner. Again, tough on everyone, but toughest on the child with autism. To a certain degree, parents can lessen the chance of big changes at the last minute by planning travel with plenty of leeway for delays, and by asking Grandma (nicely) to stick with the tried and true for one more year. But the possibility is always there that things will change unexpectedly at the last minute, wreaking havoc with the best laid plans. Consider bringing along comfort foods, clothes and videos to help your child to manage such disappointments.

Food and clothing issues, while they're difficult for any child, can be overwhelmingly difficult for children with autism.

If your family is like most, there are certain foods that everyone just loves (or at least appears to love)—and it will be hard to manage the reactions when and if your child decides that Aunt Mary's special meat loaf is slimy and nasty and just plain uneatable. There are two ways to cope with this situation: quietly and unobtrusively give your child his preferred food and murmur something about allergies and special diets, or face up to Aunt Mary and let her know that your son is absolutely right and her meatloaf is awful. Personally, I prefer method number one, but others will thank you if you select method number two.

Clothing can be an issue at family events and traditions because often major events go along with formal clothing. In today's world, formal clothing is rarely required; but at certain types of events, such as church on Christmas Eve or cousin Louie's wedding, there's no way to avoid dresses, suits, and nice shoes.

Sam H. at King Richard's
Renaissance Fair in Carver, MA

We've learned to compromise on the issue of clothing. First, we select the clothes to be worn early on, so that they're not new on the big day, and we've already removed any offending labels. Second, we say "yes" to easy, simple fixes to problematic clothing. For example, Tom will happily wear slacks, belt, and button-down shirt—but insists on rolling up the sleeves. Granted, he "should" be wearing a jacket and tie, with buttoned cuffs. But if he looks presentable, feels comfortable, and is behaving well, it's close enough for jazz.

One other major issue that should probably be mentioned is real and/or presumed family judgments. If your child's cousins are decked out in their Sunday best while your child is wearing sneakers, or your sister's child is showing off her straight As while your child is barely squeaking through social skills class, or your mother gives you The Look when your autistic daughter forgets to say "please" and "thank you"—it hurts. In fact, having a child with special needs, no matter how much you love and are proud of that child on a day-to-day basis, suddenly becomes a much bigger deal when you're under the spotlight. Not only does everyone else see every flaw, but so do you.

One Christmas, our whole family got together at my parents— brother, sister, cousins, aunts, uncles—but we spent almost the entire weekend hiding out in the playroom with the door shut, while Tom simply avoided everyone. From time to time, he'd pop his head out—at which point the whole family would turn, smile, and make welcoming noises. Tom, who, of course, was immediately overwhelmed by the attention, would turn tail and flee. It was not a happy weekend. I'm happy to say that was many years ago—and today Tom is far more capable of enjoying a family get-together (though he's still unlikely to hang out with a large gang as they chatter, laugh, and joke).

Of course, the feelings you may have, whether embarrassment, frustration, anger, or self-consciousness, are very real. And the causes may be just. But it may help to remember that your cousin, sister, and niece are probably having similar feelings, even if for different reasons. In fact, there are entire books and reams of magazine articles written about the trauma of holiday stress. And those books and articles are written not for the parents of children with special needs but for everyone.

One lesson we've learned from spending holidays with our families is that the "issues" are not only yours or your child's. If your father just can't stand being around a child who makes odd noises or your sister rolls her eyes whenever she sees your son "stimming," the fault is neither yours nor your child's. Of course, you can take the time to prepare your family for your child, provide them with a list of "do's" and "do nots," and be sure your child's favorite foods, videos, toys and blankets are available. All that may help. But in the long run, if your family is less than supportive, your child is not the sole reason.

On the other hand, if you avoid holidays with family altogether for fear of judgment, both you and your child may be missing out on something quite special. It can be both surprising and rewarding when you discover than your autistic child has a talent or interest in common with cousin Kate or that your mother-in-law has a tremendous talent for engaging your child in reading, chatting, or board games.

Clubs and special-interest groups

Many people with autism have special interests that become all-consuming. Among the most common are trains, Lego, superheroes and comics, sports statistics, graphic novels and Manga, collecting (of almost anything), and games like Dungeons and Dragons, Second Life, and chess. Teachers and therapists tend to call these special interests and passions "perseverations" or "obsessions" and treat them as either eccentricities to be quashed or as "reinforcers" to be offered as rewards for behaving ever more typically.

To those people who also engage in these or other areas of interest, though, your child's passion and level of knowledge are not only acceptable but very welcome indeed. And while your child's absolute obsession with, say, Japanese Manga, may seem odd to you, to other Manga fans it's as welcome as a day in spring. Your child's intimate knowledge of certain video games may make him "weird" to his soccer-playing peers, but to video gamers it's absolutely normal. In fact, bottom line, your child with autism may well have a group of dear friends just waiting to be found.

Sometimes, kids with autism have parents who are, at bottom, very similar to their autistic kids. Just like their children, some parents really are enthralled by train spotting, fascinated by football stats, or addicted to Dungeons and Dragons. If such is the case, it should be easy for you to find a group that will welcome your child and his interests. In fact, you may find that attending a model-train club as a parent–child team not only makes it easy for your child but also provides you with an outlet for an area of special interest.

If, on the other hand, your child's interests are alien to you, you'll have to make a special effort to learn more about her interests and to seek out clubs, groups, and opportunities for your child to share her passion with people who will understand, relate to, and value her interests. Where do you find such groups?

SCHOOL

Many schools have after-school clubs that focus on areas of interest including comic-book drawing, animation, videography, and other subjects that are often of interest to kids with autism. Depending on your child's functional level, you may need to shadow him during after-school activities (or, perhaps, the school can provide an aide to support your child).

COMMUNITY CENTERS

Many community centers are open to having teens take part in activities such as chess, photography, birding, astronomy, and so forth. Granted not many teens take advantage of the opportunity, but your child may be more than welcome.

COLLEGES AND UNIVERSITIES

Your child may be old enough to take part in programs that take place at local community colleges or universities. From environmental action groups to reading programs, there's something out there for most people.

Science and technology

Even at a very young age, it's common for kids with autism to have a special affinity for science, technology, math, and engineering. Your child may have few social skills but be able to build extraordinary structures from building toys like K'Nex or Lego. She may have a fascination for robotics, an amazing capacity to take apart and fix mechanical devices, or an innate skill with computers.

No, these abilities and interests aren't "typical." But on the other hand, they're not as unusual as you may imagine. What's more, they're tremendous stepping stones on the way to finding opportunities of all sorts—from competitions to internships to college scholarships. Your child with autism may or may not be ready to join a science-and-technology-oriented group; if the interest is there but the social skills are not, you can always begin at home with kits that allow your child (with your help) to build skills like reading a blueprint, operating a motor, using software to create an animation, and much more. As he can manage the social and communications challenges, you can introduce your child to programs available through schools, universities, and libraries that build on an intrinsic interest in computers, math, technology, and engineering.

Some of the more interesting options available to "techie" kids outside their own homes are offered through museums and universities interested in mentoring a new generation of scientists. Lego Mindstorms teams, for example, are often sponsored by universities. Teams of 3–10 children and an adult mentor build simple robots from Lego kits and then compete to see whose robot does the best job at completing selected tasks. Other possibilities (many of interest to both parents and children) include:

Cubby Elder, age 18, learning to repair automobile transmissions as an apprentice at his dad's company

- amateur astronomy clubs
- ham-radio clubs
- model-airplane and model-rocket clubs
- after-school engineering clubs
- online gaming clubs
- public-access television stations
- science camps and vacation schools.

Through groups like these, kids meet like-minded children and adults, find friends and mentors, and build a positive sense of self. What's more, they discover that their atypical interests are not off-the-wall but are merely unusual—and that there's an international community of intelligent, creative people who share their interests and abilities. More information about where and how to find science-and-technology clubs and activities is available in Appendix 3.

Amusement parks and Disney World

You wouldn't ordinarily expect to find a child with autism at an amusement park. And you may, very reasonably, choose not to take your child to a place where the crowds can be overwhelming, the lines can be long, the rides can produce sensory overload, the food is questionable—and the likely outcome is a very expensive meltdown.

All that said, we have had some absolutely terrific experiences at amusement and theme parks with our son on the autism spectrum. The key is to choose your destination wisely, to go when the crowds and heat are at their lowest ebb, and to have a Plan B if Plan A (run around like a nut and get on every crazy ride you can) doesn't work out just as you expected.

Another important tip: be sure to call ahead of time to find out whether the park offers accommodations for special needs. Many do offer "head-of-the-line" passes for kids likely to fall apart while waiting; others may have special hours or events. Of course, you'll also want to prepare your child for the experience with photos and a plan of action (often you can find photos and maps on the park's website).

While our family is not addicted to amusement and theme parks, we do enjoy them. And we have discovered that there are parks and there are parks. The typical amusement park (in the U.S., the big chain is called Six Flags) is big, ugly, loud, and great fun for typically developing people aged about 11 to 25. For most other people—autistic or not—they're just not a ton of fun.

But there are atypical amusement parks. Places designed with families in mind, where magical themes come to life, rides take many forms (not just fast and furious), shade and relaxation are available, and kids with special needs are accommodated. While I refer, of course, to the Disney parks (much more on this later), I can also highly recommend two Pennsylvania theme parks: Hershey Park and Knoebels.

Hershey is a traditional theme park, created by—you guessed it—Milton Hershey, creator of the famous Hershey Bar. And yes, it's really in Hershey, Pennsylvania. And yes, Hershey, Pennsylvania, really does smell like chocolate, and there really is a ride through a pretend "chocolate factory"—which our son just loves.

What makes the park a great destination for our family is the fact that there are such a range of experiences and places available. Some kids with autism will really go for the sensory input of the roller coaster—but many (like Tom) find it overwhelming. So while our daughter and her dad enjoy the high-energy roller coasters, Tom and I can take a gentle, stress-free ride on a "sky glider" (essentially a gondola). We can look down and watch the fish in the pond, look up and watch the screaming roller-coaster riders, and enjoy the fact that we're *not* getting twisted into pretzels by a high-gravity loop-the-loop. Hershey also has a full-scale zoo (Tom loves zoos), a dolphin show (who doesn't love dolphins?), and a reasonable selection of foods.

Knoebels is a very old-fashioned amusement park in a little town called Elysburg, Pennsylvania. At this park, the family tradition is strong, the rides are old-fashioned, and the lines are short. It's one of many such small, old-fashioned, family-style amusement parks. Ask around: you may find that families in your neighborhood know of "secret" parks (Knoebels is among the many well-kept secrets that only local folks know about) that will become your favorite destination.

Jon and Alex at Knoebels
Amusement Park in Pennsylvania

Disney theme parks and the child with autism

Amazingly, the subject of Disney World (or the older Disneyland) and autism has been addressed many times, in many locations. You'll find that Kathy Labosh has written a whole little book on the subject, including tips on where to go, what to do, and where to find the support you might need—and AllEars.net has an entire section on its site devoted to autism and The Mouse (details on these and other resources in Appendix 3). Bottom line: if you are like us and find Disney magic irresistible, there is absolutely no reason to avoid a Disney destination just because you have a child with autism. In fact, it may turn out to be a favorite destination—because (in part) of your child's autism.

First off, to call Disney World an "amusement park" is completely to misunderstand the point of the place. Yes, you can ride a few roller coasters. But that's almost by the way. Disney creates an alternate reality, where all things are as they should be. People are smiling, streets are clean, and your needs (within reason) can all be fulfilled.

If, like Tom, you think the Small World ride is just the greatest thing ever, you can know for sure that it will be the same ride, with the same music, offered in the same way, at each visit. And if, also like Tom, you dislike intense, loud rides—there are an infinite number of possible options. You can take the Liberty Belle steamboat ride into the world of Mark Twain. You can take a train ride into the Old West. You can swim among waterfalls, float down a lazy river, or nap in a lounge chair. You can meet characters—or not. You can take in a movie, a show, a game of mini-golf, a boat ride, or an afternoon at a unique arcade. The point is that no one, not even your child with autism, will find himself without an acceptable option at Disney.

Of course, there are tricks to making the Disney experience positive for a child with autism and her family. These are outlined in detail elsewhere; the basic gist, however, is as follows.

HAVE A PLAN, KNOW WHAT IT IS, AND SHARE IT WITH YOUR CHILD IN VISUAL FORM

Meanwhile, have a Plan B—the plan you'll pull out when an unexpected meltdown suddenly makes your Plan A irrelevant. Be sure that Plan B is acceptable to everyone in your party and isn't just "leave ASAP." Possibilities include retreating to the hotel for an afternoon at the pool, leaving the parks themselves and spending the afternoon canoeing or biking; etc.

KEEP YOUR PLAN LOW-KEY

"Do everything now" simply won't work well with a child who is easily overloaded or tends to be upset by changes in plan. Ideally, include at least a couple of breaks during the course of a day when your child can regroup. If necessary, allow your child to take a day or evening off with supervision.

STAY ON SITE AT DISNEY
Do this if you possibly can, so you can avoid unnecessary transitions and confusion.

PACK YOUR OWN FOOD AS NEEDED
If that's not an option, let restaurants know your needs ahead of time.

MAKE USE OF THE SPECIAL-NEEDS ACCOMMODATIONS AVAILABLE TO YOU WITH A DOCTOR'S NOTE (AND LET DISNEY KNOW YOUR NEEDS AHEAD OF TIME)
This will avoid problems with long lines and other issues.

(Note: The above information relates specifically to Disney World at Orlando, Florida. While other Disney theme parks in California, Paris, etc. have very similar rides and policies, they are not identical. It's important to check on the details—and to prepare yourself and your child—before you go.)

Family vacations
It's not unusual for families with autistic children to avoid summer vacations altogether. The idea of making so many changes all at once, combined with the stress of managing a new environment, dealing with your child's discomfort, and meanwhile attempting to "relax and have fun" can be daunting. And if family vacations actually involve extended family, the issues can get even more complex. Your child, who may be able to hold it together for an evening or an afternoon, is now subject to large-group scrutiny 24/7. It's tough on him, and even tougher on you. But there are variations to the traditional family vacation.

The staycation
When the economy took a downturn in 2008, writers coined the term *staycation*. The idea was that families could save money by staying home but acting as if they were on vacation. They'd enjoy local sights and visit local attractions but spend nothing extra on hotel or travel. In fact, staycations are often an ideal solution when you have a child with autism. That's because, while many kids on the spectrum can handle a few hours away trying something new, a week

of constant travel can be a recipe for disaster. And if something does come up while you're visiting a nearby lake or taking in a local show, it's a simple matter to decide it's just not working and go home.

The simple vacation

It took us a while to develop a solution to the family-vacation puzzle that really worked for us. We decided not to attempt to manage extended family or hotel rooms when Tom was young, but instead to rent a house near the beach. We had photos of the house and photos of the beach to share up front, as well as a plan of action that we could actually follow most of the time. Granted our vacations weren't a whirlwind of excitement, but they were relatively relaxing. We'd get up in the morning, let the kids watch television and eat sugary cereal while we relaxed on the deck with our coffee. We'd go to the beach. Come home. Eat lunch. Go to the boardwalk. Eat pizza. Come home. More TV. Bath. Bed. Repeat.

The truth is that our vacations weren't all that different from many families'. The biggest differences were the amount of advance planning (no "winging it" when it rained) and the lack of social interaction with extended family or friends. In fact, for us, a week without any input from anyone else at all was the best part of the vacation!

By the time Tom was nine, though, he was ready for more, and we felt more confident that he could handle more. We've tried camping, hotels, cities, and family visits; some have gone well, some less so. Like any family, we're still going through a process of experimentation.

The autism-friendly vacation

The world of tourism has discovered families with autism, and it's doing its very best to make a nickel off your need for a well-planned, autism-friendly holiday. If you have a little extra cash and a hankering to get away and be pampered (with your kids in tow), autism-friendly resorts and cruises may be the way to go.

I've listed some specific autism-friendly destinations in Appendix 3. But in general, you'll find there are a surprising number of possibilities available. Autism on the Seas, for example, is a travel organization that provides special autism packages aboard typical cruise ships on Princess, Disney, Royal Caribbean, and other lines. You pay the ordinary fee, but you book through this company to get:

- cruise PECS (Picture Exchange Cards – a tried and true system of nonverbal communication which involves having the child with autism trade picture cards of a desired object for the object itself)
- cruise social story (a picture-based story describing the experiences your child is likely to have during the cruise, and preparing him for surprising or unusual experiences or expectations)
- small dinner table just for your family
- all the regular services and activities on board each cruise line
- special dietary accommodations
- priority boarding onto the ship
- priority disembarkation from the ship
- private muster-drill area
- autism awareness cards for cruise staff
- access and services for people with disabilities
- professional medical physicians and nurses
- special gifts
- special potty training provisions
- special children's program grouping rules
- exemption from dinner dress code.

Basically, you get a cruise with all the comforts of a pampered vacation, while your child is cared for with a whole raft of specialized accommodations. None of this, of course, guarantees a positive experience—but it can't hurt! And, amazingly, this type of "full-service autism vacation" is becoming increasingly common. There are bed-and-breakfasts, farm holidays, and a range of other specialty vacations to choose from. The U.K.'s National Autism Society has an entire directory dedicated to autism-friendly holiday venues and organizers; you'll find details in Appendix 3.

Easy family outings

Here's a list of a few quick-and-easy outings that are likely to be successful for most families with a child on the autism spectrum. The keys to success, as always, are flexibility and a sense of humor.

THE BEACH

Always a winner, the beach knows few social expectations and includes the huge plusses of plenty of water to play in.

THE MOONBOUNCE

This American staple can be bought or rented and appears at almost every festival known to man. It's an inflatable structure inside of which children bounce. And bounce. And bounce. To many kids with autism, the moonbounce is like heaven—and outside of "no whacking," there are typically very few overt rules to worry about.

BOWLING

I have no idea why, but kids with autism seem, in general, to just love bowling. Give it a try! (Note: Most bowling alleys offer "bumpers," which make it almost impossible to throw a gutter ball. If you or your child are likely to get frustrated easily, go for the bumpers.)

THE ZOO

It's a wide open space, noise is okay, and most kids with or without autism enjoy the experience of seeing, hearing, and (sometimes) touching animals. Just be aware that strong smells and loud noises can be a problem.

THE PLAYGROUND

Kids with autism may not be as physically or socially advanced as their typical peers, but most very much enjoy swinging, sliding, and climbing. Keep an eye out to be sure their social interactions with other children go smoothly.

Ben and brothers Dan and Glenn enjoy a day at the amusement park

PUPPET SHOWS

Typically, puppet shows are brief and informal and involve broad, physical humor. Many kids with autism get a real kick out of them (as do their siblings and parents).

ANY BODY OF WATER

Kids with autism often love the water; whether it's a creek, pond, lake, or river, you'll almost certainly have a pleasant and relaxing time. Add a few boats or birds, and you're in for a terrific afternoon.

Top tips for special-interest venues and family outings

- Don't let autism stop your family from enjoying outings, events, and vacations as a family.

- The keys to ·success are careful selection, planning and preparation, accommodations, and, as always, a solid "Plan B" you can put in place quickly and gracefully.

- Try to avoid situations that are likely to place undue stress on you, your child, or the people around you. Rather than saying "I won't let autism stop me from doing what I want to do," think creatively about how to accommodate both your own interests and your child's needs and limitations.

- When dealing with extended family and family events, know that holidays and special events can be tough on everyone, not just the family with the autistic child. Do your best to accommodate your family and your child, but have a plan in mind for a graceful exit if your child (or you) start to melt down.

- Consider a wide range of possibilities for clubs, after-school activities and/or parent–child activities that accommodate your child's special interests and abilities. Your child's talent with Lego or fascination for football stats may be a terrific entrée to a club or group with similar interests and abilities.

- When planning for family vacations, make it easy on yourself and your child. Choose a setting and a plan of action that takes your child's needs into account, and have options available in case of problems. But bottom line: don't avoid vacations just to accommodate your child's desire for sameness!

Chapter 11

Selling the Idea of Inclusion

You're sold on the idea of getting out and exploring with your autistic child. Your child with autism is thriving in the settings you've found for him. But it's not at all unusual for an organization or community leader simply to turn you away at the door, saying, "We don't have the facilities/ability to handle your child's needs." It's even more common to hear, "Your child is welcome to give it a try, but we can't change our program/facility to meet special needs." In other words, if your child can magically become "unautistic," he's welcome to be included. But if he actually has the needs you describe, it just won't work out.

It is perfectly reasonable to say to such organizations, "If you don't want us, we don't want you," and walk away. But if you have a real interest in opening doors for your child with autism (and others children and families with similar issues), this is a good time to take action. A rising awareness of and incidence of autism mean that almost everyone knows or knows of someone with autism. And that, in turn, means that kids with autism are no longer simply "people with disabilities": they're the children, grandchildren, neighbors, or nieces of a great many nonprofit board members, church leaders, community leaders, and elected officials. If you're so inclined, the time is ripe to sell inclusion.

The cash factor

As I've mentioned in earlier chapters, most community organizations are nonprofits. Nonprofits live on a combination of individual donations, grants, and membership or ticket sales. Families with autistic children can have a very large impact on all these income sources, in various ways.

To begin with, if we use the most recent number from the CDC, something like 1 in 100 children is diagnosed with autism—and those children are growing up. If there are six million people in New York City, then in theory something like sixty thousand people are or will be diagnosed with autism. Assume that each of those individuals is part of a family that includes three additional individuals, and you're looking at a quarter of a million people who are out there seeking not only services and therapies but also social activities, creative programs, and places of worship. Assume that even half of those families have the time, energy, or money to give in support of organizations that make them feel welcome, and it's easy to see why there might be an incentive to reach out to families with autistic members.

Think about it: would you be more likely to make a donation to the church, synagogue, sports organization, or museum that went out of its way to include your child, or the one that didn't? Multiply your donation by 100,000 in New York alone. Then add in the donations and tickets given and purchased by doting grandparents, friends, school groups, and other interested individuals and groups. You can see that families with autism have some real potential to add to (or subtract from) the bottom lines of supportive organizations.

Families with autistic members are an increasingly important group to consider. But direct ticket sales and donations are only a small part of the financial package. For many organizations, a much bigger chunk of the annual budget comes not from individuals but from foundations. Federal agencies and major foundations give very large grants—up to multiple millions over several years—in support of programs and projects that meet their guidelines. These days, an increasingly large percentage of foundations are turning their gaze toward autism.

It doesn't take a great deal to make an organization or program "autism friendly." In fact, it's a relatively low-cost, low-impact "fix" and much less expensive than the legally required ADA accommodations for individuals with physical disabilities. Here are the basics:

- A photographic and/or video preview of the program and/or facility.

- A quiet space that's available to families with autistic children on an as-needed basis (very similar to areas now available in some institutions for nursing mothers).

- Staff training in recognizing autistic behaviors and accommodating the needs of people with autism.

- Occasional quiet or "special" times when families with autism can take part in programs without worrying about sensory overload or the judgments of other parents.

Of course, there are a thousand additional services, programs, and opportunities that can make experiences richer, more rewarding, and more significant for kids with autism and their families. But just the basics, as listed above, are enough. And even added together, the amount of time, money, and energy required is relatively low.

Meanwhile, the grant money supports not only the program for people with autism but also part of the salaries of people who are receiving training, for the people who handled the photography/ videography (which can be used for all kinds of marketing and outreach in addition to serving the needs of the autistic population), and even for part of the cost of running a building if special events are provided.

Once an organization has opened itself up to families with special needs, it can then use its newfound openness as a tool for additional fundraising. Photos and testimonials from families who have gained through the organization's autism awareness and programming can be very powerful fundraising tools, as can images of children and teens with autism successfully achieving significant goals, performing on stage, and otherwise doing well and flourishing in the community. If you received a piece of direct mail showing and telling you about a fabulous, inclusive, family program in your area, wouldn't you be likely not only to attend but also to consider making a donation when the annual appeal came around? The same marketing approach that works well with families can also be effective in reaching out to local businesses, banks, and family foundations. One autism-friendly program, cleverly leveraged, could lead to a very significant increase in donations.

It's also worth pointing out that, in some cases, a major accomplishment by an individual with autism has resulted in positive national and international publicity for an organization. "J Mac," the autistic youth who won a basketball game for his team, became a major hero, and he and his school became the subject of a movie. AMC Cinemas is gaining positive publicity for its willingness to present "sensory-friendly" showings of first run movies.

Overcoming objections to inclusion

In some cases, the mere smell of money is enough to move an organization to take action. A parent points out grants available to make programs accessible and—pow!—the organization is on it. Sometimes that quick movement forward is precipitated by a powerful board member who hears of the opportunity, thinks of an autistic grandchild, and decides to champion the cause. Similarly, organizational members—from coaches to church deacons to Cub Scout leaders—may have a personal connection to autism, and hearing that cash is available to improve accessibility, they're ready to take action.

In other cases, it's just not that simple.

A few reasons that organizations won't seriously consider inclusion are the following.

FEAR

They've read about some awful thing that a person with autism did, and they sure as heck don't want it happening here.

ANXIETY

They're not sure they can cope with disabilities, so why open that can of worms?

SNOBBISHNESS

They run a high-end program, and they really have no interest in reaching out to individuals who may not be able to keep up with their awesomeness. (In this case, of course, they may not be aware that the autistic child they just turned away could, in fact, be a prodigy!)

IGNORANCE
Many people assume that it will require a huge effort or a great deal of money to make their programs accessible to kids with autism.

BAD EXPERIENCES
They once included a child with autism, and it was a disaster. Or his mother made their lives a misery. Or they were suddenly overrun with children with autism. And they don't want to run the risk of a repeat experience.

LACK OF INTEREST
They have 50 things on their plate, and accessibility to anyone with a disability is number 51.

Most of the time, these issues disappear with education. Organizations need to know that there's cash available to support accessibility (and that training and materials used for accessibility can be repurposed for other needs). They need to understand that autism does not mean the same thing as incompetence and that many people with autism not only can succeed but even shine in their field. They need to know that children with autism are very different from one another (as are their mothers). As to the issue of being overrun with autistic children—what an opportunity!

The biggest issue, bar none, is lack of interest. When an organization is a nonprofit, has a mission that includes accommodating people of all backgrounds and abilities, understands the financial and institutional plusses that can come with inclusion but still says "it's not for us," you can be pretty sure it's a lost cause. The only way to move such an organization forward is through personal interaction with members of its top leadership. If that's not possible, quite frankly, it's time to walk away.

How to sell inclusion
Armed with statistics, knowledge, and (ideally) a personal relationship with the chairman of the board, the church deacon, the head of the sports league, or the mayor, all you need is a short list of available

local grants (easily accessible through Google), and you're ready to take action. If you're not personally connected with anyone in a leadership capacity, chances are that someone in your local parent group or support group is. If no one you know has a connection, check in with your autism-oriented therapists and teachers at school and/or at autism agencies and clinics. Someone out there will know someone who matters.

Make an appointment with the organization's leadership—but at the same time, ask that the person who will be presenting, organizing, or managing inclusive programs be present. In that way, you can answer questions and cope with objections all at once. More importantly, you're likely to find the person who works "in the trenches" with kids and parents has much more knowledge of and experience with autism than the leadership realizes. For example, museum directors may never see a child with autism, but you can bet that museum educators not only see but also work with such children and their parents every day. The same may go for pastors and religious-school teachers; recreation-department managers and coaches; drama-school administrators and drama teachers; and so forth.

Show up with at least one other person—another parent, a teacher or therapist, a board member. Present yourself with a firm, professional but friendly demeanor. You're not here to beg, cajole, or threaten: you're here to present information and opportunities that will enrich the organization in many ways. Start by making your case. Essentially, your job is to point out the following facts:

- There are X number of families in the organization's service area that would like to attend/be part of the organization if it were more accommodating of the needs of people with autism.

- Autism is not as scary as they might imagine (provide a short primer on the breadth of the autism spectrum and the talents/abilities of many people with autism).

- Meeting the needs of children and teens with autism is easier and less expensive than they think (you can share the list above).

- There are grants available to support accommodations (share your short list).

- The positive publicity they can generate through an inclusion program will reflect well on them and result in both increased membership/ticket sales and grants/donations.

- You are personally able/willing to help with the process. Depending on your background, experience, and available time, you may be able personally to offer:

  1. *cash.* Yes, there are some individuals who are wealthy enough to plunk down the money needed to start up a program.

  2. *practical support.* You may be able to help in the process of designing, running, or creating materials to support accommodation. If you're a photographer, videographer, Web designer, teacher, fundraiser, public-relations writer, etc., there's a lot you can do.

  3. *perform outreach.* You can offer to be the point person to reach out to the local autism community, letting them know of new programs or opportunities available.

Answer any questions that may be raised, either by the leadership or by the "trenches" person in the room. As mentioned, you may find the "trenches" person is a true ally: he or she has almost certainly worked with autistic kids in the past, and it's likely that the experiences were positive. In some cases, in fact, autism may be a daily fact of life in the trenches and support from management would be a fabulous way to improve the overall quality of the program.

Assuming that the meeting goes well, you might want to point out how great it is that the organization is thinking positively about inclusion since their mission specifically mentions it! As you conclude your meeting, be sure you know what will happen next. *Do not leave* without a commitment of some sort: a next meeting time, a punch list for action, a timeline, or some other clear plan for working toward inclusion. See the grant proposal in Appendix 2 for suggestions on setting a timetable.

After you leave, shoot a memo to everyone involved—and to your personal list of supporters—letting them know what happened and where you're headed. Ask your own supporters to send notes to the organization, letting them know how delighted they are to hear of plans for autistic inclusion, and how excited they are to take part in future programs.

Of course, as with any project, the devil's in the details. Everything will depend on your ability to manage the process that you've begun. But if you've ever managed a project and people—from a church potluck to a major international conference—you have the skills and tenacity to move things forward.

Bonne chance!

Selling inclusion to yourself, your friends, your family, and your child

If you're raising a child with autism, you're probably tired much of the time. Your spouse or partner is probably pretty weary, too. Your autistic child is not likely to offer you much in the way of enthusiastic, energetic support. What that means, sometimes, is that you may feel that all this work is just too much.

Even if you yourself are permanently upbeat and energetic, it's highly likely that you'll run into resistance from time to time. Whether it's your mother telling you you're not providing enough discipline, your child whining on the way to a "fun" event, or your child's teacher telling you that your child once again failed to line up properly for recess, someone will do his or her best to take the wind out of your sails.

When that happens, it's easy to decide that getting out, exploring, and having fun sounds lovely—but it's just too much to manage. After all, your life is full enough without going through the process of coping with difficult community leaders or coaching your autistic child in swimming skills.

My personal method for managing feelings like these is pretty simple.

First, I complain, loudly and bitterly, in a very private setting. That seems to take the edge off. Next, I have a glass of wine and a little something tasty—or take a long walk to a lovely location. Last, I give myself permission to decide that I'm doing absolutely nothing for my child with autism for the next hour, afternoon, evening, or however long I think I need. And I don't.

From time to time, I simply let things drop. Yes, I thought it'd be a great idea to help X organization develop programs and funding to accommodate my child and others—but quite frankly, it's too much work right now, and it's not important enough in the greater scheme of things.

But when the feelings of exclusion, frustration, or sheer exhaustion get to be too much, I'm always fairly sure that my energy and positive outlook will return—not because I'm such an upbeat, cheery person (though I sometimes am) but because I've had enough success over time know that I'll succeed again. And so will my son.

Have fun!

Top tips for promoting inclusion

- Be aware that most nonprofit institutions have a mission that states that they are open to all, regardless of race, gender, or ability.

- Know that accommodating families with autism is not a massive undertaking: institutions need not spend enormous sums of money or extraordinary amounts of time to become autism-friendly.

- Understand that, for many nonprofits, including families with autistic children can be a great boon. It opens the doors to positive publicity, increased fundraising opportunities, more donations, and more ticket sales.

- When approaching any nonprofit, come prepared with information, fundraising opportunities, and an existing relationship with someone in power at the organization.

- Take an active role in promoting inclusion, by helping as you can with the processes of fundraising, promotion, marketing, or management.

- When you get tired, frustrated or furious (and you will), take a step back. Take a break. Know that your child's future is not dependent upon your ability to get a particular group or organization excited about inclusion.

- Most importantly, remember that you and your family are neither powerless nor unimportant. With some strategic planning and creativity, you can make a tremendous impact on the world in which your child is growing up.

Appendix 1

A General Guide to Autism for Community Leaders

As with the tip sheets in previous chapters that could be photocopied and shared with teachers, coaches, or clergy, the general guide on the following pages may also be copied and handed out to community and youth leaders who will be working with children or teens on the autism spectrum.

If you do make use of this guide, be sure that community leaders know you intend to be available to help with planning, troubleshooting or support as necessary. You might even consider providing your community leader with tools for accommodating your child or a group of children with autism. For example, you may want to provide specialized art equipment that meets your child's special needs (e.g., glue sticks, specialized scissors, etc.), rather than expecting the community leader to source and purchase such supplies.

I've also found it helpful to actually set up times to chat with the community leader about how things are going. I'll make a point not only to ask about my own child's progress, but also to ask about any issues that may be arising for either the leader or the other children. By bringing up the questions myself, I make it easier for the leader to express her real observations; otherwise, I've found, leaders may simply tell me "he's doing great," and avoid providing me with the details I need to support true success. In the long run, I've found that open lines of communication are key not only to my child's success but also to building long-term relationships with community leaders and organizations.

✓

A General Guide to Autism for Community Leaders

If you have years of experience working with children in your community, chances are very good that you have years of experience working with autistic children. The autism spectrum is very broad and includes kids who are profoundly disabled and nonverbal, as well as kids who are bright, verbal—but somehow different. If you've worked with a child who had a hard time reading social cues, interacting with other kids, or talking about anything other than his own favorite subject, there's a good chance that child could have an autism-spectrum diagnosis.

Now that autism is better understood, there are lots of kids out there with autism-spectrum diagnoses. If you're asked by a parent to include his or her child with autism in a program, sports team, activity, or event, you'll need to know something about the disorder and to have some ideas for helping that child take an active, successful part in the experience you're leading.

The word *autistic* is very vague. Children with autism vary radically. Some are loud, some are quiet, some are very bright, and some are mentally retarded. The child you're including in your program is unique, so it's important to know as much as you can about him or her before you get started. To find out about the child, you can:

- ask parents to chat with you and/or fill out a questionnaire
- request a copy of the child's Individualized Education Program (IEP) if he or she is at school
- meet with the child's teacher and/or aide
- meet with the child
- observe the child at home or at school
- ask the child to come for a visit.

What you're looking for are clues to let you know about the child's strengths and interests, what accommodations the child might need, what challenges may emerge, and how best to handle any problems as they arise.

Strengths and interests

Kids with autism often have extraordinary strengths and passionate interests. Even if a child with autism has a tough time with social interactions or fine-motor projects, she may be a whiz at keeping track of scores, managing equipment, reading aloud, and so forth. Parents, teachers, and the kids themselves may be able to share this information with you or to suggest opportunities for building on the child's strengths.

Accommodations

Often, kids with autism overreact to ordinary sights, sounds, or actions. They may also have a tough time following verbal directions. It's usually easy to accommodate those issues if you can plan ahead. For example, if a child has a tough time with sticky, gooey craft items, you can provide him with a glue stick instead of a bottle of liquid glue or with clay rather than papier-mâché. If a child needs visual cues, you can work with his parents to create a picture-based schedule or plan. If a child has a tough time knowing when and where to pass a ball, you can practice during off hours or let his parents know what skills to work on.

Challenges and solutions

What might happen when you include a child with autism? Most likely, you'll have a terrific addition to your program, organization, or event. But what if something comes up? Here are some of the most likely issues that will come up with a child on the spectrum and some potential solutions.

DIFFICULTY FOLLOWING SPOKEN INSTRUCTION

Many kids with autism have difficulty following spoken directions. If you're accustomed to talking to your group for several minutes at the start of your program or event and expect kids to remember what you've said, you'll run into trouble if you don't provide extra support to your member with autism.

An easy fix is to provide written and/or visual directions that say the same things as your spoken instructions. You can write up a list of instructions (for example, "First, find and put down the newspaper;

next, gather your paint and brush," etc.), you can provide pictures of the activity step by step, or you can ask the child's parents to do this ahead of time (be sure to give parents clear instructions and plenty of time to do this). Alternatively, you can ask a member of the group to partner with your autistic group member to help out.

Another good option for instructing a child with verbal challenges is hand-over-hand instruction, which involves placing your hand over the child's and directing his movements. This is a great way to teach "muscle memory" for activities such as karate or yoga moves, dance, baseball, and so forth. (Do check with parents before physically guiding a child with autism. The child may respond poorly to being touched, or prefer a certain type of physical interaction.)

LACK OF FOCUS

Many kids with autism have a hard time staying focused on a leader who is making a presentation.

An easy fix is to place the child at the front of the class or group, include her in a demonstration, or ask her to help you out by handing out materials, acting as a model, etc.

PHYSICAL LIMITATIONS

Some kids with autism have fine- and gross-motor delays. This can make it tough, for example, to kick or throw hard and accurately, to cut with scissors, to write in cursive, and so forth.

When you encounter this kind of situation, you have two choices. You can either accommodate the child's challenges by, for example, doing some cutting for him or placing him in positions that require less strength and accuracy, or you can work with him to build skills. Both of these are good choices, but if you do decide to work on skills, be sure you have the time and patience available.

SENSORY ISSUES

Many, but not all, people with autism over- or underreact to sensory input. Bright louds, loud noise, sticky sensations, certain tastes or smells can either overwhelm them or get them overexcited.

Be sure to ask your group member's parents about any such issues—and ask, too, for suggestions as to how to accommodate or manage those concerns. In most cases, it's fairly easy to, for example, turn down the lights, avoid blowing a whistle loudly near the child's ears, or substitute a glue stick for sticky paste.

Sometimes, though, there's no way around the sensory issues: band practice will always be loud, swimming will always be wet, and coaches do need to blow whistles some of the time. If possible, prepare the child for these issues (by telling him in advance that they'll be happening) and plan for them together. It might be possible for the child to wear a pair of sound-muffling earphones or even to cover his ears when a loud noise is coming.

ODD MOVEMENTS OR NOISES

It's not unusual for a child with autism to "flap" her hands, pace, or make odd noises (grunts, giggles, etc.). These are referred to as "stims," and often they help the child to manage her own physical or emotional responses.

If there's no good reason for the child to stop stimming (for example, if it's not too loud or too disruptive, etc.), there's no reason to do anything at all about it.

If it does become an issue, however, you may want to give the whole group a chance to wiggle and move around and then ask the child with autism to limit herself to quiet movement after that. You may also want to offer her options that are more appropriate to the setting (for example, "It's okay to pace, but not to giggle"; "It's okay to squeeze this fidget toy, but not to drum on the table").

EMOTIONAL IMMATURITY

Kids with autism may appear to be old enough to manage their feelings, but very often frustration can become overwhelming. It may be surprising and even concerning to see a 12-year-old suddenly dissolve into tears.

Be sure to ask your group member's parents about any emotional issues that might arise and get their direction on how to manage such issues when they do come up. Some kids may do very well with a short time away from the group; others have comfort objects like squeezy balls or toys that help them calm down. Still others may need to call it a day and head home.

✓

DIFFICULTY MAKING FRIENDS

One of the greatest challenges for kids with autism is in making friends. There are really two separate issues to consider: first, the child with autism himself and, second, the rest of your group.

While the child with autism may not want to be close buddies with anyone (and some kids just don't), it is important that she behave appropriately with her peers. Most children with autism are perfectly capable of following basic group rules (being quiet when the leader is speaking, raising hand to speak, etc.).

If you find that some of her behaviors are out of hand (she's spitting, hitting, etc.), you're absolutely within your rights to separate her from the group and have a conversation about the issues with her parents and/or an organizational supervisor. If the issues can't be resolved, and there's no one-on-one aide available to help manage the issues, it may make sense to ask the child to leave the group.

Similarly, the typical children in your group are under no obligation to be best friends with a child with autism. They should, however, be supportive and kind. You might want to brainstorm with parents ahead of time to decide how (or whether) to discuss a special need or to recommend special rules of behavior with the rest of the group.

You may also find that there are kids within your group who would enjoy and be good at mentoring your autistic group member. If one or two kids seem like good "buddy" material, it makes good sense to encourage it. Two words of caution, though: (1) It's important that a typical buddy understand that it's not his job to do everything *for* the child with autism; instead, it's his job to explain or help as needed. (2) It's important to keep an eye out to be sure the buddy is still getting his fair share of opportunities to shine within the group, or to complete his own projects.

Always and never

While kids with autism are as different from one another as any other group of kids, there are some simple rules of thumb to follow to help your group member to thrive.

Always

- Assume that your group member with autism will be able to take part in your activities at some meaningful level.
- Keep the bar high. It's tempting to say "Great job!" when a disabled child does anything at all, but if you know he can do more or better, let him know!
- Think creatively about teaching methods, peer buddying, accommodations, and innovative ways to keep your group member involved and having fun.
- Keep the lines of communication open between yourself and the child's parents. The more they know, the more they can help.
- Tap parents as needed. They can be experts, volunteers, group parents, or even one-on-one aides.

Never

- Assume that your group member with autism is stupid or incompetent.
- Allow other group members to bully or tease a child with autism (or anyone else, for that matter).
- Allow a child with autism to bully or tease anyone else.
- Allow a child with autism simply to zone out and avoid participating altogether.
- Allow a child with autism to disrupt your program or make it impossible to complete the project you have in mind. If necessary, get parents involved to ensure that everyone in the group has a positive experience.

Remember

Everyone in your group has challenges and talents. As a youth leader, it's your job to help kids overcome their challenges and fulfill their potential. You may find that it's particularly rewarding to work with a child with autism—your leadership is critical to his success, and his success can mean everything to him and his family.

Appendix 2

Sample Grant Proposal

Every funding agency will have slightly different guidelines for grant proposals. This short proposal, with some additions and tweaking, successfully raised over $20,000 over two years for an inclusive YMCA day-camp program in 2005 and 2006. It first offers a general introduction to the topic, stressing the need for the program in the community, then details the aims of the program, and presents a timetable to enact the steps needed for completion. Of course, it is most important that you specify how much grant money you are seeking.

Sample Grant Proposal

Summer, when most children are enjoying time with their friends at camp, is particularly difficult for children diagnosed with high-functioning autism, Asperger syndrome, ADD, and ADHD. While these children may shine academically, significant difficulties in social, communications, and motor skills mean they are often unable to participate in typical summer-camp activities. Yet summer is an ideal time to focus specifically on social, communication, and physical skills and to practice them intensively in a fun, social, nonacademic setting. In the metropolitan Philadelphia area, there is no summer-camp program available specifically for AS/ADHD children.

A group of area parents, in cooperation with the Philadelphia YMCA, is developing Camp Outlook, a summer program for July 2004, to serve the needs of AS/ADHD children. Camp Outlook will offer both inclusive and specialized activities in a day-camp setting. The goals of the program include:

- creating a pilot program to offer an opportunity for approximately 20 children ages 6 through 12 with an AS/ADHD diagnosis to take part in an exciting, enriching summer camp at a metropolitan Philadelphia YMCA

- providing opportunities for AS/ADHD children to be included in the YMCA's morning-camp program with the support of trained one-on-one aides

- creating and implementing an afternoon program offering therapeutic activities in the areas of drama, recreation, and science

- evaluating the success of the program with the goal of improving and expanding it (at an additional YMCA location) for summer 2005.

WINTER 2003–04

Program partners, including parents, YMCA staff, therapists at Temple University and Chester County Intermediate Unit, and educational consultants will work together during the winter to develop a program, schedule, and admissions criteria.

JANUARY–SPRING 2004

Parents across the region will be informed of the camp program and asked to apply for admission. Two groups of children will be selected, ages 6–9 and 10–12. Staff will be recruited and trained. Evaluation will begin.

SUMMER 2004

In July 2004, approximately 20 children will attend the pilot summer-camp program. Evaluators will observe, interview, and measure gains among children attendees and will interview parents and staff.

FALL/WINTER 2004–05

The program team will review evaluations, refine the camp program, and plan for an expanded camp program in July 2005.

We are requesting a grant of $___ toward a total of $15,000 in seed money to support program development, planning, marketing, and evaluation. Additional program costs, including therapeutic support and program implementation, supplies, and space rental will be covered by an appropriate per-child fee. Fundraising for camp scholarships will begin in fall 2004.

Appendix 3

Resource List

Chapters 1, 2, and 3: General information

FRAMES OF MIND: THE THEORY OF MULTIPLE INTELLIGENCES
by Howard Gardner (Basic Books 1993)
This seminal book explains the idea that there are different types of intelligences and provides insights into how children learn differently.

ALL KINDS OF MINDS: A YOUNG STUDENT'S BOOK ABOUT LEARNING ABILITIES AND LEARNING DISORDERS
by Mel Levine (Educators Publishing Service, Inc. 1992)
In this book, Mel Levine changed the way many people think about education. The title says it all: each child learns in a unique manner and may need to be taught differently.

ENGAGING THE CHILD WITH AUTISM: USING THE FLOORTIME APPROACH TO HELP CHILDREN RELATE, COMMUNICATE AND THINK
by Stanley Greenspan and Serena Wieder (DeCapo Press 2006)
This most recent book about the floortime approach to play therapy for children with autism is a practical guide for parents.

DISCOVERY TOYS
www.discoverytoysinc.com/web/guest/autism
Includes marble mazes, construction toys, and other autism-friendly items, which are actually coded for learning styles. In addition, you

can sort through this company's catalog for toys that specifically build cooperation, support sensory needs, and so forth.

BRIO TOYS
http://brio.knex.com
Thomas the Tank engines, track, and accessories, K'Nex building toys, Lincoln Logs as well as many other attractive, tough toys are available through Brio. (Note: Many of these same toys are available gently used on Ebay or at yard sales for a fraction of the retail cost.)

CAROL GRAY'S SOCIAL STORIES™
http://thegraycenter.org
Whether you go with stories created by Carol Gray or by one of her many followers (or create social stories yourself) these picture-based narratives have proved their usefulness for kids on the autism spectrum. Social stories provide a verbal and visual preview or review of experiences, feelings, expectations, and so forth, and provide information about how to meet one's own and others' needs. For example, "When I get ready for church I put on a tie. If I can't tie it myself, I can ask Dad for help," etc.

MODEL-ME KIDS®
http://modelmekids.com
This series of videos and supporting activity books and lesson plans are visual tools for teaching social skills, communication skills, non-verbal body language, and more.

Chapter 4: Sports
SPECIAL OLYMPICS
www.specialolympics.org
Special Olympics is an international organization dedicated to providing "year-round sports training and athletic competition in a variety of Olympic-type sports for children and adults with intellectual disabilities, giving them continuing opportunities to develop physical fitness, demonstrate courage, experience joy and participate in sharing of gifts, skills and friendship with their families, other Special Olympics athletes and the community."

EASTER SEALS

www.easterseals.com/site/PageServer?pagename=ntl_camping_
and_recreation_sports
This organization offers a wide range of athletic and recreation
programs to individuals with disabilities.

VARIETY CLUB

www.varietyclub.org.uk
This well-established charity offers a wide range of programs and
opportunities to kids with disabilities. Depending upon where you
live, the local Variety Club may offer great sports opportunities.

TOPSOCCER

www.usyouthsoccer.org/programs/topsoccer/index_E.html
U.S. Youth Soccer TOPSoccer (The Outreach Program for Soccer) is
a community-based training and team placement program for young
athletes with disabilities, organized by youth soccer-association
volunteers. The program is designed to bring the opportunity of
learning and playing soccer to any boy or girl, ages 4–19, who has a
mental or physical disability.

CHALLENGER BASEBALL

www.littleleague.org/Learn_More/About_Our_Organization/
divisions/challenger.htm
The Challenger Division was established in 1989 as a separate division
of Little League Baseball to enable boys and girls with physical and
mental challenges, ages 5–18 or the completion of high school, to
enjoy the game of baseball along with the millions of other children
who participate in this sport worldwide.

POP WARNER CHALLENGER FOOTBALL LEAGUE

www.popwarner.com/images/PWChal.pdf
The Challenger Program is a noncompetitive program; no score is
kept. The games are modeled after a typical Pop Warner game with
warm-ups, coin toss, etc. Participation in the Challenger division is
permitted at the request of the individual's parent or guardian.

SPECIAL HOCKEY INTERNATIONAL

www.specialhockeyinternational.org

Special Hockey allows the developmentally challenged to achieve their own goals on their own schedule.

Chapter 5: Youth groups and organizations

BOY SCOUTS OF AMERICA

www.scouting.org

Read up on today's Boy Scouts and find packs and troops near you.

WORKING WITH SCOUTS WITH DISABILITIES

www.wwswd.org

This website links to a wide range of resources for Boy Scout leaders and parents to support boys with autism and other disabilities.

GIRL SCOUTS OF AMERICA

www.girlscouts.org

Find out what the organization is all about and how it serves girls with all types of abilities.

WORLD ASSOCIATION OF GIRL GUIDES AND GIRL SCOUTS

www.wagggsworld.org; www.wagggsworld.org/en/projects/wagggs_network/share/40

Read about Girl Guides and Girl Scouts around the world; get detailed information including contact information for including girls with disabilities.

4-H

www.4-h.org

This website will open your eyes to the American extension program that started out with a special focus on farmers and now embraces all Americans with an incredible range of programs.

JOURNAL OF EXTENSION

www.joe.org

The searchable website of the *Journal of Extension* provides all kinds of interesting studies and examples of 4-H programming for kids with autism and related disabilities.

YMCA

www.ymca.net

Find a Y near you; learn about Y programs. Check out www.ymca. net/adventureguides/ for details on the Y's Adventure Guide youth club program. Search the YMCA site for information about accommodations and programs for kids and teens with disabilities.

CAMP FIRE USA

www.campfireusa.org

Yes, they were the Camp Fire Girls. But now they're co-ed and offer girl, boy, co-ed, and family programs, groups, and camps.

Chapter 6: Museums, zoos, and aquariums

There's no way to know whether your local museum, aquarium, zoo, or botanical garden is accessible or appropriate for your child with autism—except to ask. Here's where to find listings for your local cultural, arts, or nature center. Once you find the right listing, call and ask for information, resources, and contacts.

CHILDREN'S MUSEUMS

www.childrensmuseums.org

SCIENCE MUSEUMS

www.astc.org

ART MUSEUMS

www.artcyclopedia.com/museums.html

ZOOS AND AQUARIUMS

www.aza.org

NATURE CENTERS IN THE U.S.

www.eeweek.org/nature_centers.htm

PUBLIC GARDENS IN THE U.S.

www.publicgardens.org

BOTANIC GARDENS INTERNATIONAL

www.bgci.org

Chapter 7: Faith communities

Non-denominational

DISABILITY SOLUTIONS

www.disabilitysolutions.org/newsletters/files/one/1-4.pdf

An entire Disability Solutions newsletter on religious inclusion.

AUTISM AND FAITH: A JOURNEY INTO COMMUNITY

http://rwjms.umdnj.edu/boggscenter/products/documents/
AutismandFaith.pdf

Download this entire booklet, which includes a wealth of articles, resources, and information about worship and autism.

INTERFAITH DISABILITY CONNECTION

www.interfaithdisability.org

Interfaith Disability Connection educates and engages faith communities in cultivating mutually beneficial relationships with people with challenges, including autism.

JONATHAN'S CHILD, INC.

www.jonathanschild.com

This is a special-needs ministry dedicated to the spiritual health of children and adults with autism and to all who love a special-needs child.

Attending Catholic services

THE NATIONAL APOSTOLATE FOR INCLUSION MINISTRY

www.nafim.org

The National Apostolate for Inclusion Ministry has created an entire website that offers tips and ideas for including developmentally disabled individuals at Mass and in Sunday school.

ARCHDIOCESE OF NEWARK DISABILITIES

www.rcan.org/index.cfm?fuseaction=category.display&category_id=96

The Pastoral Ministry with Persons with Disability site offers a wealth of resources.

THE NATIONAL CATHOLIC PARTNERSHIP ON DISABILITY
www.ncpd.org
Rooted in Gospel values that affirm the dignity of every person, the National Catholic Partnership on Disability (NCPD) works collaboratively to ensure meaningful participation of people with disabilities in all aspects of the life of the church and society.

Attending Evangelical services
THE CHRISTIAN COUNCIL ON PERSONS WITH DISABILITIES
www.ccpd.org
This site offers support, resources, and ideas for Evangelical churches interested in including persons with developmental disabilities.

Attending mainstream Protestant churches
THE RELIGION & SPIRITUALITY DIVISION OF THE AAIDD
(American Association on Intellectual and Developmental Disabilities)
www.aaiddreligion.org
The AAIDD offers a variety of resources to share with individual churches to promote inclusion. Its services include a certification program for pastors, a newsletter, annual conferences, and more.

ENABLE-DISABILITY
www.fbjb.com/ministries/enable_disability.php
The mission of enABLE is to share God's love by providing opportunities of Baptist worship, fellowship, respite, and personal growth to people with developmental challenges such as autism and their families.

UNITED CHURCH OF CHRIST DISABILITIES MINISTRIES (UCC-DM)
www.uccdm.org
"Accessible to All" is their motto.

Attending Jewish services

THE NATIONAL JEWISH COUNCIL FOR THE DISABLED

www.perceptions4pcople.org/component/content/article/77-general/101-national-jewish-council-for-the-disabledyachad-.html?directory=2

This site offers conferences, camps, programs, curricula, and classes. Children can prepare for Bar and Bat Mitzvah, take part in youth programs, and become fully included in Jewish life.

UNITED SYNAGOGUE OF CONSERVATIVE JUDAISM

www.uscj.org/Accessibility7508.html

Website offering information and resources for inclusion.

PRAYING WITH LIOR

www.prayingwithlior.com

The website for the documentary film *Praying with Lior*, about a boy with Down syndrome preparing for his Bar Mitzvah.

THE FRIENDSHIP CIRCLE

www.fcnj.com

The Friendship Circle extends a helping hand to families who have children with autism and other special needs and involves them in a full range of Jewish and social experiences.

JEWISH FAMILY SERVICE

www.jfsbergen.org

This organization works to strengthen and preserve the well-being of individuals and families; to help them effectively meet the challenges and changes through life by providing quality human services and professional counseling to all who call upon its services.

Attending Muslim services

AL NOOR AUTISM AWARENESS

http://alnooraa.webs.com/mission.htm

Al Noor Autism Awareness (ANAA) is an international organization working to develop and maintain a global community of caring, unified, and knowledgeable individuals in an effort to support individuals with autism along with their families and friends, especially for the Islamic community.

HUMANITARIAN RESPONSE TO PEOPLE WITH DISABILITIES (HRD)
www.masjids.org
Imam Furqan Muhammad, the resident imam at Masjid Al-Muminun in Atlanta, advocates for the inclusion of people with challenges in the Islamic community. Imam Muhammad currently serves as a member of the Board of the Interfaith Disability Connection.

AUTISM AND THE GOD CONNECTION
by William Stillman (Sourcebooks, Inc. 2006)
An intriguing exploration of autism and spirituality.

Chapter 8: Visual and performing arts
Autistic artists' galleries
AUTISM SOCIETY OF AMERICA AUTISM ART GALLERY
www.autism-society.org/site/PageServer?pagename=art_exhibit

STEPHEN WILTSHIRE'S ONLINE GALLERY
www.stephenwiltshire.co.uk
Wiltshire is a true artistic savant.

DONNA WILLIAMS'S ART AND AUTISM SITE
www.donnawilliams.net/artandautism.0.html

Art therapy organizations
These websites provide detailed information about the purpose and practice of arts therapies, along with directories that allow you to search for qualified therapists in your area.

AMERICAN ART THERAPY ASSOCIATION
www.arttherapy.org

NATIONAL ASSOCIATION FOR DRAMA THERAPY
www.nadt.org

AMERICAN DANCE THERAPY ASSOCIATION
www.adta.org

AMERICAN MUSIC THERAPY ASSOCIATION
www.musictherapy.org

Additional arts resources

VSA ARTS
www.vsarts.org
An international nonprofit organization celebrating the power of the arts in the lives of individuals with disabilities.

ART LESSONS AND ACTIVITIES FOR KIDS
www.princetonol.com/groups/iad/lessons/middle/for-kids.htm

THE MIRACLE PROJECT
www.themiracleproject.org
An organization that provides help with involving kids with autism in production of musical shows.

INTERNATIONAL DIRECTORY OF SCULPTURE GARDENS
www.sculpture.org/documents/parksdir/world.shtml

ACTING ANTICS: A THEATRICAL APPROACH TO TEACHING SOCIAL UNDERSTANDING TO KIDS AND TEENS WITH ASPERGER SYNDROME
by Cindy B. Schneider and Tony Attwood (Jessica Kingsley Publishers 2006)
A useful tool for anyone thinking of starting up a drama program for kids with Asperger syndrome and high-functioning autism.

Chapter 9: Camps and the natural world

Please note that, while all these directories include day and sleep-away camps for kids with autism, they also include listings of typical camps and family camps. Enjoy!

MY SUMMER CAMPS DIRECTORY: CAMPS FOR KIDS WITH AUTISM

www.mysummercamps.com/camps/Special_Needs_Camps/
Autism/index.html

This general camp directory includes three pages of camps that are specifically geared to kids with autism-spectrum disorders. It also includes a massive listing of typical camps and family camps.

OASIS CAMP LISTINGS FOR KIDS WITH ASPERGER SYNDROME

www.udel.edu/bkirby/asperger/schools_camps.html

OASIS is a comprehensive website for Asperger syndrome, and its camp listings are fairly extensive. Be aware that OASIS does skew toward programs that are appropriate for higher-functioning kids.

VERY SPECIAL CAMPS

www.veryspecialcamps.com

Very Special Camps is a website dedicated entirely to listings of special-needs camps. They list several dozen camps around the country that are specifically dedicated to kids on the autism spectrum.

KIDS' CAMPS DIRECTORY: CAMPS FOR KIDS WITH AUTISM/ASPERGERS

www.kidscamps.com

This is another general camp directory, but it includes an impressive collection of camps and programs specifically geared to kids on the autism spectrum. It also includes a listing of family camps. Search by state.

Chapter 10: Special interests, clubs, family outings and other ideas

LEGO CLUBS

http://club.lego.com/en-us/BuildIt/FamilyDetails.aspx?id=40512

Lego isn't just for kids with autism—and Lego clubs are a very big deal. Start or join one, and you may see your child thrive.

K'NEX CLUBS

www.knex.com/club

Like Lego, K'Nex attracts its share of passionate builders, and there are clubs around the world that support their passion.

ALL THINGS RAILROAD

www.railserve.com

This incredible directory has links to absolutely everything railroad-oriented, from museums and clubs to online groups, Lego train groups, information about real train lines, magazines . . . and much more.

LABOSH PUBLISHING

www.laboshpublishing.com

These little books include hints, tips, and resources for doing various things with kids on the autism spectrum. Two of the booklets focus on vacations and Disney.

AUTISM ON THE SEAS

www.alumnicruises.org/Autism/Autism_Home.htm

Autism-friendly cruising.

NATIONAL AUTISTIC SOCIETY

www.nas.org.uk/nas/jsp/polopoly.jsp?d=1064

No matter where you're going or what you're doing in the U.K., you'll find wonderful ideas on this site. Among the buried treasures is an extensive list of autism-friendly vacation destinations in the U.K.

Index